WINNING
STRATEGIES
for
VIDEO
POKER

Lenny Frome

Compu-Flyers

5025 S. Eastern Ave. (16)
Las Vegas, NV

Published by
Compu-Flyers
5025 S. Eastern Ave.(16)
Las Vegas, NV

ISBN 0-9623766-9-3

LCCN: 93-70639

Second Edition

Printed in the United States of America

PREFACE

In 1989, we published two books on expert Video Poker strategy, for the Las Vegas and the Atlantic City machines respectively. Since then, Video Poker has spread so rapidly to many other areas that millions of new players now find the game, in its many various forms, readily available to them. Many players go to casinos wherever they travel, so they need the strategies for many unfamiliar versions of the game. Thus, it now seems timely to create a Video Poker handbook which includes accurate strategy information for the multitude of new games which players may now encounter everywhere in America.

In the earlier works, great efforts were made to demonstrate the validity of the strategies and completely justify the payback percentages which experts could attain. This approach was considered necessary to dispel any doubts about the liberality of the games offered. In this book, we have left out such data, simply because it makes all the strategies look much more complicated. The world has long since come to accept that optimal Video Poker strategies are based on a solid mathematical foundation, so that the outcome can be predicted in common probability terms.

However, the percentage payback of each machine is given, (assuming proper playing strategy) so that players can seek out the highest paybacks available in their areas. Also, each game's average Frequency of Winners is included herein, so that players might estimate the effect of playing machines which have slightly different pay tables from those explicitly shown.

We sincerely believe that all modern American Video Poker machines utilize very sophisticated random-number generators which are totally free from any external biases that could affect the outcomes, but this book does not make any claim to that effect.

i

Table of Contents

Table of Contents (continued)

INTRODUCTION

Video Poker is a popular game primarily because it pays liberally in comparison to all other slots. However, to attain these inherent high paybacks, players must learn these three points:

1. Pick the Best Machines
2. Play the Cards Right
3. Know What to Expect

To facilitate finding the best machines, we have included the top paying (full-pay) games from every locale and have identified them as such. In Nevada, it is relatively easy, since most machines are full-pay, because competition is very rough. Elsewhere, there are not many machines of Nevada caliber but players can select the "full-payers" for their own areas, while avoiding the less liberal machines. There is just no reason to believe that poor-paying machines somehow create more winners and vice versa.

Playing the cards right means playing all hands in the way which offers the highest return over the long run. Because it is virtually impossible for players to calculate mentally what all the long term returns might be for a given choice of draw (except for simple one card draws), we have done all the hard work ahead of time. To make the right draw obvious, we have made up a ranking chart for each game, listing in the totem-pole order of choice which way to play every hand. Some hands are very easy to strategize, while others, which can be played in two, three, or even four reasonable ways, must be played the highest ranking way.

Every hand in the strategy table has a numerical value assigned to it which represents its win potential. It is derived by assuming that every possible draw might come up, adding up all the payouts and dividing by the number of possible draws. Mathematically, it is the Expected Value (EV) of the pre-draw hand and is equal to the payback for that hand, e.g., an EV of 0.8 means we can expect to get only 80% back on that particular type of hand in that game with that given pay-table.

THE EV'S DO NOT HAVE TO BE MEMORIZED. They serve primarily to illustrate which hands have the most potential in each game. They also serve to point out the size of the loss caused by misplay of a hand as a lower ranking hand. The relative rankings of the hands do have to be memorized to attain best payback. Where EV's are ranked as numerically equal, they are still listed in true ranked order.

Proper use of the chart is essential to playing correctly, so we will illustrate in detail how it is utilized. Assume that we are playing the JB-1 version of Jacks or Better and we are dealt this hand,

2 ♣   3 ♥   4 ♥   5 ♥   5 ♠   [a]

which might reasonably be played in three different, reasonable ways....

(a) Hold the 4-card straight 2 ♣ 3 ♥ 4 ♥ 5 ♥ and draw 1
(b) Hold the 3-card straight flush 3 ♥ 4 ♥ 5 ♥ and draw 2
(c) Hold the pair 5 ♥ 5 ♠ and draw 3

The strategy table in JB-1, reproduced below, shows that the pair ranks higher than either of the other ways of playing the hand.

```
              JB-1 JACKS OR BETTER
           STRATEGY                  E.V.
           Royal Flush................800
           Straight Flush.............50
           4 of a Kind................25
           4 Card Royal...............18
           Full House.................9
           Flush......................6
           3 of a Kind................4+
           Straight...................4
           4 Card Straight Flush......4-
           Two Pairs..................3-
           4 Card Inside Strt Flush...2+
           Pair J's or higher.........1.5
           3 Card Royal...............1.5-
           4 Card Flush...............1.2
           4 CD Straight (3 hi cards)...0.9-
HAND (c)>>Low Pair...................0.8+
           4 CD Straight (2 hi cards)...0.8+
           4 CD Straight (1 hi card)....0.7+
           3 CD Ins Strt Flush (2 HC)...0.7+
           3 CD Strt Flush (1 hi card)..0.7+
HAND (a)>>4 CD Straight (0 hi cards)...0.7-
           3 CD DblIns Strt Flush(2 HC).0.6+
           3 CD Ins Strt Flush (1 HC)...0.6+
HAND (b)>> 3 CD Strt Flush (0 hi cards).0.6+
           2 Card Royal (KQ, KJ, QJ)....0.6+
           4 CD Ins Straight (A High)...0.6-
           2 CD Royal (A high/no 10)....0.5+
           3 CD DblIns Strt Flush(1 HC).0.5+
           4 CD Ins Strt (3 hi cards)...0.5+
           3 CD Ins Strt Flush w/0HC....0.5+
           3 High Cards no Ace..........0.5+
           2 High Cards.................0.5-
           2 CD Royal (w/10 no Ace).....0.5-
           1 High Card..................0.5-
           3 CD DblIns Str Flush (0 HC).0.4+
           RAZGU Draw 5 Cards...........0.4-
```

However, if we were dealt the same hand while we were playing some other game such as Deuces Wild (refer to DW-1), we would have two reasonable choices, three 5's or a 4-card straight flush. The DW-1 strategy table shows that this hand is best played as a 4-card straight flush, since it outranks three of a kind. Naturally, every version of Video Poker has its unique strategy table.

Thus, Deuces Wild hardly resembles Jacks or Better strategy and the strategies reflect the pay-table differences in the many variations of each game version. The very best warning that we can give is to limit the diversity of your game-playing to one or two versions, since it is well-known that players experience higher loss rates on unfamiliar games. The most costly error that players make is to play (hold) cards which should not be held. Any hand which is not listed in the table is termed RAZGU, which is another way of saying hold none, or only the bare wild cards. The second costliest error is that of holding kickers, extra cards which have no value, in fact, may reduce the value of the pre-draw hand. Thus, holding an 8 kicker with a pair of Aces is poetically correct, but extremely poor Video Poker.

Perhaps the most overlooked aspect of play is knowing what to expect. Frequency of Winners tables herein provide guidelines as to how often one can (on the average) expect any winner, so they won't expect more than what is reasonable. By studying these tables, players will not stray from their proper strategy, simply because it is not producing some improbable results. Machines can easily psych out players who fly blindly.

The Frequency Table is useful for estimating the effect on payback (%) of playing a game with relatively small variations in pay schedule with respect to one listed. For example, the Jacks or Better 8/5 game (JB-2) is sometimes seen in a 7/5 version. The loss of one bet-unit on each Full House can be estimated as causing a reduction of 1.1% in payback, since the Full House occurs about once in 90 hands.

This book is organized in sections devoted to particular versions of Video Poker, which can be found in places where gambling is legal. The games included herein are found in Nevada, New Jersey, Colorado, Minnesota, Connecticut, Wisconsin (and nearby mid-western states) and now in Louisiana and Mississippi. The tendency for each locale to have unique games is not accidental, since the prevailing laws, both written and unwritten, seem to foster specific games in that area. Luckily, almost all games in current play fall into just several major versions:

No Wild Cards (52 card deck)
Deuces Wild (4 wild-cards; 52 card deck)
Joker Wild (1 wild-card; 53 card deck)
Deuces Joker Wild (5 wild-cards; 53 card deck)
Double Joker (2 wild-cards; 54 card deck)

The strategy tables for wild-card games are sub-divided to group hands according to the number of wild cards in them. This makes it easier to learn strategy for wild card games, which generally have many more playable hands in their totem pole.

In order to facilitate recognition of the broken hands and to condense the text generally, we have created a standardized glossary of abbreviations in Appendix A. A few minutes to review this section will pay off well in actual play.

AN INVITATION: Readers are invited to submit details of any interesting games they find which are not included in, or closely related to those in this book. Be sure to identify where it was found and send a complete pay schedule for all coins played, especially if they are not simple multipliers. Give the name of the game and clear definitions of any special rules or modes which may apply. If possible, identify the manufacturer (the nameplate is usually on the side of the machine). We will give all submittals a reply and, if possible, will send a strategy for any worthwhile games. Interesting stories relating to Video Poker are always read and replied to.

Send all letters to: COMPU-FLYERS   5025 S. Eastern Ave. (16)
Las Vegas, NV 89119

This book will be a very useful companion piece to the new PC software "Video Poker Knowledge Pro" produced by Masque Publishing and available at all major software outlets. It is published only in CD-ROM format and includes all the games in this book. It also has a 26 minute video clip introducing the theory of Video Poker strategy.   PC requirements: W3.1 or W95, 486 or higher, 8 Meg RAM, SVGA 256 color monitor, 16 bit sound card and CD drive 2X or higher. MacIntosh version also available. For latest release dates and purchase info, contact Compu-Flyers.

PLAY WITH YOUR HEAD...Not Over It.

TB-1   Tens or Better

PAY TABLE Per Coin; 5 Coin Play	FREQUENCY OF WINNERS

```
Royal Flush.......800  ...  1/  39,000
Straight Flush.... 50  ...  1/   9,700
Four of a Kind.....25  ...  1/     425
Full House.........6   ...  1/      87
Flush..............5   ...  1/      95
Straight...........4   ...  1/      81
Three of a Kind.....3  ...  1/      14
Two Pairs..........2   ...  1/       8
Tens or Better.....1   ...  1/       4
Non-Winners   50%
```

PAYBACK: 99.1%

While there are still a few of these to be found around, they are definitely a vanishing breed. They are very liberal and lots of fun to play in the "Big Bertha" machine version, with their 19" or 25" screens, which permit a few players to join in community play. As competition heats up, it is likely these machines will be reborn, to again serve as eye-catching attractions to lure patrons into the casinos.

Although the Full House / Flush are only 6 / 5, the push on 10's almost offsets this reduction, while increasing the "hit frequency" to 50%, the highest available in any game. The key payline to look for is the 2 for 1 on Two Pairs, since that is often reduced to a a push on low paying versions of Tens.

TB-1   Tens or Better

```
Royal Flush................800
Straight Flush.............50
4 of a Kind................25
4 Card Royal...............18
Full House..................6
Flush.......................5
3 of a Kind................4+
Straight....................4
4 Card Straight Flush......3+
Two Pairs..................2+
Pair 10's or higher.......1.5
3 Card Royal.............1.5-
4 Card Flush...............1+
4 Card Straight  K High...0.9+
4 Card Straight  Q high...0.9-
4 Card Straight  J high...0.8+
3 Card Strt Flush  J high.0.8
Low Pair..................0.8-
4 Card Straight 10 high...0.7+
3 CD Strt Flush 10 high...0.7
4 Card Straight ..........0.7-
3 CD Ins. Strt Flush (2 HC)...0.7-
2 Card Royal Q or J high..0.6+
3 CD Dbl Ins Str Flush (2 HC).0.6+
3 CD Ins Strt Flush (1 HC)....0.6
4 CD Ins Straight (A High)....0.6-
2 Card Royal K high.......0.6-
3 CD Straight Flush (0 HC)....0.6-
2 Card Royal  A high......0.5+
3 CD Straight K or Q high.0.5+
3 High Cards no Ace.......0.5+
3 CD Dbl Ins Strt Flush (1HC).0.5
3 Card Ins Strt Flush (0 HC)..0.5
2 High Cards..............0.5-
1 High Card...............0.5-
3 CD Dbl Ins Str Flush (0 HC).0.4+
RAZGU Draw 5 Cards........0.4-
```

TB-2　Tens or Better

PAY TABLE Per Coin; 5 Coin Play	FREQUENCY OF WINNERS

```
Royal Flush.......800 ...  1/  35,000
Straight Flush.... 50 ...  1/   8,800
Four of a Kind.....25 ...  1/     430
Full House.........9 ...   1/      90
Flush..............6 ...   1/      90
Straight...........4 ...   1/      80
Three of a Kind.....3 ...  1/      14
Two Pairs..........1 ...   1/       8
Tens or Better......1 ...  1/       4
Non-Winners   51%
```

PAYBACK: 90.8%

This version is the "low-pay" game even though the Full House / Flush payouts are 9 / 6 and some unwary players may think that it's a full pay version because that combo has been on the paylines of full-pay Jacks for many years. A close look shows the Two Pair payline awarding only a push and that is a mean reduction of 12% (1 in 8 hands end as Two Pairs as shown in the Frequency table above). The bigger payouts on Full Houses and Flushes barely recover 4% since they each show up once in 90 hands.

One can only view this game as a form of amusement, best played with friends, community style, in the "Big Bertha" version. If any big hit shows up, take a walk to find something which offers a better chance to win something.

TB-2   Tens or Better

```
Royal Flush.................800
Straight Flush..............50
4 of a Kind.................25
4 Card Royal...............18+
Full House...................9
Flush........................6
3 of a Kind.................4+
Straight.....................4
4 Card Straight Flush......3.5
Two Pair...................1.7
3 Card Royal...............1.5
Pair 10's or higher........1.4
4 Card Flush...............1.2
4 Card Straight  K high....0.9+
4 Card Straight  Q high...,...0.9-
4 Card Straight  J high....0.8+
3 CD Strt Flush  J high....0.8+
4 Card Straight  10 high...0.7+
3 CD Ins Strt Flush (2 HC)...0.7+
3 CD Strt Flush 10 high....0.7+
4 Card Straight ...........0.7-
Low Pair...................0.6+
3 CD Dbl Ins Str Flush (2 HC)..0.6+
3 CD Ins Strt Flush (1 HC)...0.6
4 CD Ins Straight (A High)...0.6-
3 CD Straight Flush (0 HC)...0.6-
2 Card Royal Q or J high...0.6-
2 Card Royal K high........0.6-
2 Card Royal  A high.......0.5+
3 CD Straight K or Q high.....0.5+
3 High Cards no Ace........0.5+
3 CD DblIns Strt Flu (1 HC)....0.5
3 CD Ins Strt Flush (0 HC)...0.5
2 High Cards...............0.5-
1 High Card................0.5-
3 CD Dbl Ins Str Flush (0 HC)..0.4+
RAZGU  Draw 5 Cards........0.4-
```

PAY TABLE Per Coin; 5 Coin Play	FREQUENCY OF WINNERS

```
Royal Flush.......300 ...   1/  54,000
Straight Flush....150 ...   1/   7,000
Four of a Kind.....30 ...     1/   450
Full House........10 ...     1/    93
Flush..............8 ...     1/    60
Straight...........6 ...     1/    55
Three of a Kind....3 ...     1/    15
Two Pairs..........2 ...     2/    17
Tens or Better......1 ...    2/     9
Non-Winners   51%
```

PAYBACK: 92.4%

This version is the "high-pay" game found in Oregon, which limits the maximum payback on what they term "Video Lottery Terminals". This "cap" on payback is supposed to increase the take to the state, but it really discourages serious play and "caps" the state's income. To prove the point, the highest earning machine ever seen in Rhode Island (another "cap" state) was a Blackjack that somehow got shipped in there by mistake. It had a payback of over 97% and played to standing lines only.

Note the low Royal award.....yet another dumb product of a misguided political body. Also, note the unusual strategy that is required in view of the inflation of Straights and Flushes awards, resulting in an increase in frequencies.

TB-3   Tens or Better

```
Royal Flush.....................300
Straight Flush.................150
4 of a Kind.....................30
Full House......................10
4 Card Royal....................8+
4 Card Straight Flush...........8+
Flush............................8
Straight.........................6
3 of a Kind.....................4-
Two Pairs......................1.8
4 Card Flush...................1.6
Pair 10's or higher............1.3
3 Card Royal.(No Ace).........1.3-
4 Card Straight  K high.......1.3-
3 Card Strt Flush  J high.....1.2+
4 Card Straight  Q high........1.2
4 Card Straight  J high.......1.2-
3 Card Strt Flush 10 high.....1.1+
4 Card Straight  10 high.......1.1
3 Card Royal (With Ace).......1.1-
3 Card Straight Flush (0 HC)..1.0+
4 Card Straight ..............1.0+
3 CD Ins. Strt Flush (2 HC)...1.0+
3 CD Ins.Strt Flush (1 HC)....0.9+
3 CD Ins.Strt Flush (0 HC)....0.8+
3 CD Dbl Inst Str Flush (2 HC)..0.8+
4 CD Inside Straight (4 HC)...0.8-
3 CD Dbl Ins Strt Flush (1 HC)..0.7+
4 CD Inside Straight (2,3 HC)...0.6+
3 CD Dbl Ins Strt Flush (0 HC)..0.6+
3 High Cards no Ace...........0.6+
3 Card Flush (2 HC)............0.6
4 CD Inside Straight (1 HC)...0.6-
Low Pair......................0.6-
2 Card Royal..................0.6-
3 Card Straight (Jack high)...0.5+
4 Card Inside Straight (0 HC)..0.5
3 Card Flush (1 HC)............0.5
2 Card Straight Flush (1 HC)...0.5
2 High Cards..................0.5-
2 CD Inside Strt Flush (1 HC)..0.5-
1 High Card...................0.5-
3 Card Flush (0 HC)............0.4
2 Card Straight Flush (0 HC)..0.4-
RAZGU Draw 5 Cards............0.3+
```

JB-01   Jacks or Better

PAY TABLE Per Coin; 5 Coin Play	FREQUENCY OF WINNERS

```
Royal Flush.......800 ...   1/  40,400
Straight Flush.....50 ...   1/   9,200
Four of a Kind.....25 ...      1/   425
Full House.........9 ...       1/    87
Flush..............6 ...       1/    91
Straight...........4 ...       1/    89
Three of a Kind....3 ...       1/    14
Two Pairs..........2 ...       1/     8
Jacks or Better....1 ...       1/     5
Non-Winners   55%
```

PAYBACK: 99.5%

This version is the original "full-pay Jacks"which turned Video Poker from an oddity to America's National Game of Chance. It is the **MUST LEARN** game for all players since it (a) is liberal, (b) is learned easily, (c) teaches hand recognition, (d) is the baseline for a multitude of "Bonus" games which followed, is only moderately volatile, and (e) is fairly accurate if used on other games (8/5, 7/5) offered everywhere, the figures being the Full House /Flush pays.

Players can easily judge how liberal a casino's VP's are by observing what pay table the Jacks games are offering. If there are "full pay" Jacks machines, it is likely to be offering many liberal games. *Warning*: Don't assume all 9 / 6 pay tables are liberal; check the two-pair payline also!

JB-01 Jacks or Better

```
Royal Flush...................800
Straight Flush................50
4 of a Kind...................25
4 Card Royal..................18+
Full House....................9
Flush.........................6
3 of a Kind...................4+
Straight......................4
4 Card Straight Flush.........4-
Two Pairs.....................3-
4 Card Inside Strt.Flush......2.4
Pair J's or higher............1.5
3 Card Royal..................1.4
4 Card Flush..................1.2
4 Card Straight (3 HC)........0.9-
Low Pair......................0.8+
4 Card Straight (2 HC)........0.8
4 Card Straight (1 HC)........0.7+
3 CD Ins Strt Flush (2 HC)....0.7+
3 CD Straight Flush (1 HC)....0.7+
4 Card Straight (0 HC)........0.7-
3 CD Dbl Ins Strt Flush(2 HC)..0.6+
3 CD Ins Strt Flush (1 HC)....0.6+
3 Card Strt Flush (0 HC)......0.6+
2 Card Royal (KQ, KJ, QJ).....0.6+
4 CD Inside Straight (4 HC)...0.6-
2 Card Royal (A high/ no 10)..0.5+
3 CD Dbl Ins Strt Flush(1 HC)..0.5+
3 CD Ins Strt Flush (0 HC)....0.5+
4 Card Inside Strt (3 HC).....0.5+
3 High Cards no Ace...........0.5+
2 High Cards..................0.5-
2 Card Royal (w/10 no Ace)....0.5-
1 High Card...................0.5-
3 CD Dbl Ins Strt Flush (0 HC).0.4+
RAZGU Draw 5 Cards............0.4-
```

JB-02   Jacks or Better

PAY TABLE
Per Coin; 5 Coin Play

FREQUENCY OF WINNERS

Royal Flush.......800	...	1/ 40,200
Straight Flush.....50	...	1/ 9,300
Four of a Kind.....25	...	1/ 425
Full House.........8	...	1/ 87
Flush..............5	...	1/ 92
Straight...........4	...	1/ 89
Three of a Kind....3	...	1/ 14
Two Pairs..........2	...	1/ 8
Jacks or Better.....1	...	1/ 5
Non-Winners 55%		

PAYBACK: 97.3%

This is the version that is "high pay" Jacks in locales where casinos have minimum competition. In Las Vegas it is the game in bars, laundromats and supermarkets. Since it also is very widely played with a Progressive Jackpot on Royal Flushes, this strategy is applicable when the Jackpot is near its minimum reset value (800 for 1). For the case where the Jackpot has doubled, see JB 03.

Note that the 8 / 5 (Full House / Flush) paylines reduce the payback by 2.2%, which translates to an increase of 6X the loss rate, compared to a 9 / 6 machine. If you see only 8 / 5 's in a casino, you can be pretty sure the other games offered are not liberal. Your best bet is to wait for an "overdue" progressive (even 7/ 5) to be available.

14

JB-02   Jacks or Better

```
Royal Flush................800
Straight Flush.............50
4 of a Kind................25
4 Card Royal...............18+
Full House.................8
Flush......................5
3 of a Kind................4+
Straight...................4
4 Card Straight Flush......4-
Two Pairs..................3-
4 Card Inside Strt Flush...2+
Pair J's or higher.........1.5
3 Card Royal...............1.5-
4 Card Flush...............1+
4 CD Straight (3 Hi Cards).0.9-
Low Pair...................0.8+
4 Card Straight (2 HC).....0.8+
4 Card Straight (1 HC).....0.7+
3 CD Ins Strt Flush (2 HC).0.7
3 Card Strt Flush (1 HC)...0.7-
4 Card Straight (0 HC).....0.7-
3 CD Dbl Ins Strt Flush (2 HC).0.6
3 CD Ins Strt Flush (1 HC).0.6
3 Card Strt Flush (0 HC)...0.6
4 Card Inside Straight (4 HC)..0.6
2 Card Royal (KQ,KJ,QJ)....0.6
2 Card Royal (A high/no 10)..0.5+
4 Card Inside Strt (3 HC)..0.5+
3 High Cards no Ace........0.5+
3 CD Dbl Ins Strt Flush(1 HC)..0.5
2 High Cards...............0.5-
3 Card Ins Strt Flush (0HC)..0.5-
2 Card Royal (w/10 no Ace)..0.5-
1 High Card................0.5-
3 CD Dbl Ins Strt Flush (0 HC).0.4+
RAZGU Draw 5 Cards.........0.4-
```

JB-03   Jacks or Better

PAY TABLE Per Coin; 5 Coin Play		FREQUENCY OF WINNERS	
Royal Flush	1,600 ...	1/	32,700
Straight Flush	50 ...	1/	9,300
Four of a Kind	25 ...	1/	425
Full House	8 ...	1/	87
Flush	5 ...	1/	90
Straight	4 ...	1/	90
Three of a Kind	3 ...	1/	14
Two Pairs	2 ...	1/	8
Jacks or Better	1 ...	1/	5
Non-Winners 55%			

PAYBACK: 99.5%

Here, we have "frozen" the Progressive meter at 1,600 for 1, a payout of $2,000 on quarters ($8,000 on dollar games), a point where the game is equivalent to a "full pay" 9/6, but still not giving the player an advantage. The game would be "positive" at $2,200 provided the player is just as "positive" about actually hitting the Royal.

The strategy on Progressives is ever changing as the meter moves up and down. One can see that the partial Royals move up the strategy table and as a result the hit frequency on Royals drops to 1 in 32,700 from 1 in 40,000 on a "flat top" machine. Chasing Royals is for the pros, for to be good at the sport, one must learn how to adjust the strategy constantly to suit the meter...a tough business.

JB-03 Jacks or Better

```
Royal Flush............... 1,600
Straight Flush............... 50
4 Card Royal................. 35+
4 of a Kind.................. 25
Full House................... 8
Flush........................ 5
3 of a Kind.................. 4+
Straight..................... 4
4 Card Straight Flush........ 4-
Two Pairs.................... 3-
4 Card Inside Strt Flush..... 2+
3 Card Royal................. 2+
Pair J's or higher........... 1.5
4 Card Flush................. 1+
4 Card Straight (3 HC)....... 0.9-
Low Pair..................... 0.8+
4 Card Straight (2 HC)....... 0.8+
4 Card Straight (1 HC)....... 0.7+
3 CD Ins Strt Flush (2 HC)... 0.7+
3 CD Straight Flush (1 HC)... 0.7+
4 Card Straight (0 HC)....... 0.7-
2 Card Royal (KQ,KJ,QJ)...... 0.6+
2 CD Royal (A high/no 10).... 0.6+
3 CD Dbl Ins Strt Flush (2 HC).0.6+
3 CD Ins Strt Flush (1 HC)... 0.6+
3 Card Strt Flush (0 HC)..... 0.6+
4 Card Ins Straight (4 HC)... 0.6-
4 Card Ins Straight (3 HC)... 0.5+
3 High Cards no Ace.......... 0.5+
2 Card Royal (w/10 no Ace)... 0.5+
2 Card Royal (A-10).......... 0.5
3 CD Dbl Ins Strt Flush(1 HC).0.5
2 High Cards................. 0.5
3 CD Ins Strt Flush (0 HC)... 0.5
1 High Card.................. 0.5-
3 CD Dbl Ins Strt Flush (0 HC).0.4
RAZGU Draw 5 Cards........... 0.4-
```

JB-04   Jacks or Better

PAY TABLE Per Coin; 5 Coin Play		FREQUENCY OF WINNERS	
Royal Flush	1,000 ...	1/	36,100
Straight Flush	50 ...	1/	9,200
Four of a Kind	25 ...	1/	425
Full House	6 ...	1/	87
Flush	5 ...	1/	90
Straight	4 ...	1/	91
Three of a Kind	3 ...	1/	14
Two Pairs	2 ...	1/	8
Jacks or Better	1 ...	1/	5
Non-Winners 55%			

PAYBACK: 95.5%

This is the low-pay game that is usually offered in new jurisdictions, but which gives way to more liberal games as the competition heats up. It was the main game (other than jokers) in A.C. for many years and there are still many nickel machines there.

The strategy is fairly accurate when applied to 6/ 5 Bonus games and those are found in many locales. It's a tough machine to ever beat without a strong rush of Quads, so playing the partial Royals is expecially important. Note the way the 3 Card Royal has jumped above the High Pair and don't miss the opportunities to capitalize on two card Royals. Hint: Ace and Ten (2 Card Royals) also play if no discards must be made in same suit.

18

JB-04 Jacks or Better

```
Royal Flush................1,000
Straight Flush.................50
4 of a Kind...................25
4 Card Royal................22+
Full House.....................6
Flush..........................5
3 of a Kind..................4+
Straight.......................4
4 Card Straight Flush.........4-
Two Pairs.....................3-
4 Card Inside Straight Flush....2+
3 Card Royal................1.7
Pair J's or higher..........1.5
4 Card Flush................1.1
4 Card Straight (3 HC).........0.9-
4 Card Straight (2 HC).........0.8+
Low Pair......................0.8+
4 Card Straight (1 HC).........0.7+
3 Card Ins Strt Flush (2 HC)....0.7+
3 Card Straight Flush (1 HC)....0.7+
4 Card Straight (0 HC).........0.7-
3 CD Dbl Ins Strt Flush (2 HC)..0.6+
2 Card Royal (KQ,KJ,QJ)........0.6+
3 CD Ins Strt Flush (1 HC)......0.6+
3 CD Straight Flush (0 HC)......0.6+
4 CD Inside Straight (4 HC).....0.6-
2 Card Royal (A high/no 10).....0.5+
4 Card Inside Straight (3 HC)...0.5+
3 High Cards no Ace...........0.5+
3 CD Dbl Ins Strt Flush (1 HC)..0.5
2 High Cards..................0.5
3 CD Ins Strt Flush (0 HC)......0.5
2 CD Royal (w/10 no Ace).......0.5-
1 High Card...................0.5-
3 CD Dbl Ins Strt Flush (0 HC)..0.4
RAZGU Draw 5 Cards...........0.4-
```

JB-05   Jacks or Better

PAY TABLE Per Coin; 5 Coin Play		FREQUENCY OF WINNERS	
Royal Flush.......800	...	1/	42,000
Straight Flush.....50	...	1/	9,200
Four of a Kind.....80	...	1/	425
Full House..........8	...	1/	90
Flush...............6	...	1/	90
Straight............4	...	1/	90
Three of a Kind.....3	...	1/	14
Two Pairs...........1	...	1/	8
Jacks or Better.....1	...	2/	9
Non-Winners 55%			

PAYBACK: 98.5%

Called Bonus Poker DeLuxe, it's not quite so de-luxe in payback but offers a quick recovery from any losing session with its mini-jackpot on Quads. This "generosity" is made possible by trimming the Two Pair payline to a push, but apparently BDeL players want the chance to win big or lose fast and don't care about time on the machines.

A key to the strategy is the role of the Low Pair, so you must seize all of your opportunities to score on Quads.

Players are warned that there are many machines out there called by the same name, but offering only 5 on Flushes. Even the dollar machines employ this bit of deception, so the lesson is: you have to watch the Pay Table, not the decorative glass.

JB-05 Jacks or Better

```
Royal Flush.................800
4 of a Kind.................80
Straight Flush..............50
4 Card Royal................18+
Full House..................8
3 of a Kind.................6+
Flush.......................6
Straight....................4
4 Card Straight Flush.......4-
4 CD Inside Strt Flush......2+
Two Pairs...................1.6
Pair J's or higher..........1.5
3 Card Royal................1.5
4 Card Flush................1.2
4 Card Straight (3 HC)......0.9
Low Pair....................0.8+
4 CD Straight (2 Hi Cards)..0.8+
4 Card Straight (1 HC)......0.7+
3 Card Ins Strt Flush (2 HC)..0.7
3 Card Strt Flush (1 HC)....0.7
4 Card Straight (0 HC)......0.7-
3 CD Dbl.Ins Strt Flush(2 HC)..0.6+
3 CD Ins Strt Flush (1 HC)..0.6+
3 CD Straight Flush (0 HC)..0.6
4 CD Inside Straight (4 HC)..0.6
2 Card Royal (KQ,KJ,QJ).....0.6-
2 Card Royal (A high/no 10)..0.5+
4 CD Inside Straight (3 HC)..0.5+
3 CD Dbl Ins Strt Flush(1 HC)..0.5+
3 CD Ins Strt Flush (0 HC)..0.5
3 High Cards no Ace.........0.5-
2 High Cards................0.5-
2 CD Royal (w/10 no Ace)....0.4+
1 High Card.................0.4+
3 CD Dbl Ins Str Flush (0 HC)..0.4
RAZGU Draw 5 Cards..........0.3+
```

JB-06   Jacks or Better

PAY TABLE Per Coin; 5 Coin Play		FREQUENCY OF WINNERS	
Royal Flush.......800 ...		1/	40,200
Straight Flush.....50 ...		1/	9,400
4 of a Kind.(A's)..80 ...		1/	5,200
(2-3-4's) 40		1/	1,900
(5 - K's) 25		1/	610
Full House.........8 ...		1/	87
Flush..............5 ...		1/	92
Straight...........4 ...		1/	89
Three of a Kind.....3 ...		1/	14
Two Pairs..........2 ...		1/	8
Jacks or Better.....1 ...		1/	5
Non-Winners 55%			

PAYBACK: 99.2%

This is the original Bonus Poker, which I believe was created either to offset the overly liberal paybacks offered in the Deuces Wild series, (over 100%) or to lure players from the full-pay 9/ 6 Jacks with their 99.5% payback. In any case it has worked perfectly and has since led to a myriad of "bonus" games which are extremely popular.

Bonus Pokers award bigger payouts on Quads in exchange for 8/5 paylines (Full House/ Flush). This makes the game more volatile than Jacks with a minor payback reduction. The award on 2-3-4's tames the payback but generates a bit of excitement when these small pairs show up. The more liberal Aces and Faces rewards the higher Quads.

JB-06   Jacks or Better

```
Royal Flush...................800
Four Aces.....................80
Straight Flush................50
Four 2,3,4s...................40
Four 5 to Ks..................25
4 Card Royal.................18+
Full House.....................8
3 of a Kind (Aces)...........  .6+
Flush..........................5
3 of a Kind (2,3,4)...........5-
3 of a Kind (5 to K)..........4+
Straight.......................4
4 Card Straight Flush.........4-
Two Pairs.....................3-
4 Card Inside Straight Flush....2+
Pair Aces....................1.7
Pair J's - K's..............1.5+
3 Card Royal.................1.5
4 Card Flush.................1.1
4 Card Straight (3 Hi Cards)....0.9-
Low Pair (2-10)..............0.8+
4 Card Straight (2 HC)........0.8+
4 Card Straight (1 HC)........0.7+
3 CD Inside Strt Flush (2 HC)...0.7
3 Card Straight Flush (1 HC)....0.7
4 Card Straight (0 HC)........0.7-
3 CD Dbl Ins Strt Flush (2 HC)..0.6
3 CD Inside Strt Flush (1 HC)...0.6
3 Card Straight Flush (0 HC)....0.6
4 Card Inside Straight (4 HC)...0.6
2 Card Royal (KQ,KJ,QJ).......0.6-
2 Card Royal (A high/no 10)...0.6-
4 Card Inside Strt (3 HC).....0.5+
3 High Cards no Ace...........0.5+
2 High Cards...................0.5
3 CD Dbl Ins Strt Flush (1 HC)..0.5
3 Card Ins Strt Flush (0 HC)....0.5
2 Card Royal (w/10 no Ace)....0.5-
1 High Card...................0.5-
3 CD Dbl Ins Strt Flush (0 HC)..0.4
RAZGU Draw 5 Cards...........0.4-
```

23

JB-07 Jacks or Better

PAY TABLE Per Coin; 5 Coin Play		FREQUENCY OF WINNERS	
Royal Flush.......800	...	1/	45,000
Straight Flush.....50	...	1/	6,000
4 of a Kind.(A's).160	...	1/	4,900
(2-3-4's) 80		1/	2,200
(5 -K's) 50		1/	720
Full House.........8	...	1/	105
Flush..........25	..	1/	42
Straight...........4	...	1/	115
Three of a Kind.....3	...	1/	16
Two Pairs..........1	...	1/	10
Jacks or Better.....1	...	2/	11
Non-Winners 60%			

PAYBACK: 134 %

Too good to be true? No, it's true, but you must play this game called **Flush Attack** only when the Attack is "ON" so you will be paid 25 for 1 on Flushes. And you must follow this strategy, which increases the Flush frequency to 1 in 42 or the other players in the Shared Hit Linkage will get a Flush before you and cause the Attack to go "OFF".

Some machines are not linked, so you don't have to rush, but don't get on the machine unless it's "ON" or you know <u>at least one 5-coin Flush was hit</u> on it (in "OFF" mode) before you started. Then, you can expect your Attack to go "ON" after you hit two more 5-coin Flushes. Your loss rate will be 13% in between Attacks, so the risk is high.

JB-07   Jacks or Better

```
Royal Flush.................800
4 Aces......................160
Four 2-3-4's................80
Straight Flush..............50
Four 5-K's..................50
Flush.......................25
4 Card Royal................22-
3 Aces......................10-
Full House..................8
Three 2-3-4.................7-
4 Card Straight Flush.......6+
4 CD Inside Strt Flush......6-
Three of a Kind (5-K).......5+
4 Card Flush................5-
Straight....................4
3 Card Royal................2+
Pair A's....................1.7
Two Pairs...................1.6
Pair of Faces (J,Q,K).......1.5-
3 Card Straight Flush.......1.4+
3 Card Ins Strt Flush.......1.4-
3 CD Dbl Ins Strt Flush.....1.3
3 Card Flush................1.2
4 Card Straight (2,3 HC)....0.8+
Pair..(2-3-4)...............0.8
2 Card Royal (No 10)........0.7+
4 Card Straight (1 HC)......0.7+
Pair.(5-10's)...............0.7
4 Card Straight (0 HC)......0.7-
2 Card Royal (incl. 10).....0.6+
4 Card Ins Strt (3,4 HC)....0.6
2 Card Flush w/ Ace.........0.6-
2 Card Flush w / 1HC........0.6-
1 Ace (discard Other Face)..0.5
1 High Card (Bar 2 HC)......0.5
3 High Cards no Ace.........0.5-
2 Card Flush................0.4
No RAZGU Hands
```

JB-08   Jacks or Better

PAY TABLE Per Coin; 5 Coin Play		FREQUENCY OF WINNERS	
Royal Flush.......800	...	1/	40,200
Straight Flush.....50	...	1/	9,400
4 of a Kind.(A's). 80	...	1/	5,100
(K-Q-J's) 40		1/	1,700
(2-10's) 25		1/	610
Full House.........8	...	1/	87
Flush..............5	..	1/	92
Straight...........4	...	1/	89
Three of a Kind.....3	...	1/	13
Two Pairs..........2	...	1/	8
Jacks or Better.....1	...	2/	9
Non-Winners 55%			

PAYBACK: 99.3 %

Aces and Faces is the name Binion's applied to this game which is still proprietary to the Horseshoe in downtown Las Vegas. With an added Sequential Royal award at 10,000 for 1, this game heralded the Bonus Pokers boom, as players were willing to sacrifice a bit of payback for the shot at a big win, or at least a chance for a quick recovery from a cold session.

Although we will play more pairs of Faces than pairs of low cards like 2, 3, 4's, the increase in overall payback vis-a-vis Bonus Poker (JB 06) is barely 0.1%. however the key play is holding a high pair vs. a 3-card Royal. When the Sequential Royal is offered, it adds 0.2% to payback.

JB-08   Jacks or Better

```
Royal Flush.................800
Four Aces....................80
Straight Flush...............50
Four J,Q,Ks..................40
Four 2-10s...................25
4 Card Royal................18+
Full House....................8
3 of a Kind (Aces)...........6+
Flush.........................5
3 of a Kind (J,Q,K)..........5-
3 of a Kind (2 to 10)........4+
Straight......................4
4 Card Straight Flush........4-
Two Pairs....................3-
4 Card Inside Straight Flush....2+
Pair Aces or Faces..........1.7
3 Card Royal Flush.........1.4+
4 Card Flush...............1.2
4 Card Straight (3 Hi Cards)....0.9
Low Pair (any)............0.8+
4 Card Straight (2 HC)....0.8+
4 Card Straight (1 HC)....0.7+
3 CD Inside Strt Flush (2 HC)...0.7+
3 CD Straight Flush (1 HC)....0.7+
4 Card Straight (0 HC)....0.7-
3 CD Dbl Ins Strt Flush (2 HC)..0.6+
3 CD Inside Strt Flush (1 HC)...0.6+
3 Card Straight Flush (0 HC)....0.6+
4 Card Inside Straight (4 HC)...0.6·
2 Card Royal (KQ,KJ,QJ).........0.6-
2 Card Royal (A high/no 10).....0.5+
3 CD Dbl Ins Strt Flush (1 HC)..0.5+
3 Card Ins Strt Flush (0 HC)....0.5+
3 High Cards no Ace............0.5+
4 Card Inside Straight (3 HC)...0.5+
3 CD Dbl Ins Strt Flush (1 HC)..0.5
2 High Cards...................0.5-
2 Card Royal (w/10 no Ace)......0.5-
1 High Card....................0.5-
3 CD Dbl Ins Strt Flush (0 HC)..0.4+
RAZGU Draw 5 Cards.............0.4-
```

JB-09   Jacks or Better

PAY TABLE Per Coin; 5 Coin Play		FREQUENCY OF WINNERS	
Royal Flush.......800	...	1/	40,200
Straight Flush.....50	...	1/	9,300
4 Aces (Prog've) 80	...	1/	5,100
Eights (Prog've) 80	...	1/	5,700
Sevens..........50	...	1/	5,700
2-6; 9- Kings....25	...	1/	500
Full House.........8	...	1/	87
Flush..............5	..	1/	91
Straight...........4	...	1/	89
Three of a Kind.....3	...	1/	14
Two Pairs..........2	...	1/	8
Jacks or Better.....1	...	1/	5
Non-Winners 55%			

PAYBACK: 99.7 %

Known as Aces and Eights, this game is proprietary to the Circus properties. It was an early entry into what has become the "bonus poker" boom. It is among the most liberal games since the two progressives are included only at minimum reset values (80) in the payback estimate. Furthermore, a Sequential Royal (not shown above) adds another 0.2% to the attraction.

With this array of Progressive Jackpots, there's lots of color and action. Add all the jugglers and trapeze artists overhead plus the assorted circus acts and you have everything any serious Video Poker player could wish for.

28

JB-09   Jacks or Better

```
Royal Flush...................800
Four Aces or Four 8's.........80
Straight Flush................50
Four 7's......................50
Four of a Kind................25
4 Card Royal..................18+
Full House.....................8
3 of a Kind (Aces or 8's)......6+
3 of a Kind (7's)..............5+
Flush..........................5
3 of a Kind ...................4+
Straight.......................4
4 Card Straight Flush..........4-
Two Pairs......................3-
4 Card Inside Strt Flush.......2+
Pair Aces......................1.7-
Pair J-Q-K.....................1.6-
3 Card Royal...................1.4+
4 Card Flush...................1+
Pair 8's/ 7's..................1-
4 Card Straight (3 Hi Cards)....0.9-
Low Pair (any).................0.8+
4 Card Straight (2 Hi Cards)....0.8+
4 Card Straight (1 Hi Card).....0.7+
3 CD Inside Strt Flush (2 HC)...0.7+
3 Card Straight Flush (1 HC)....0.7+
4 Card Straight (0 HC).........0.7-
3 CD Dbl Ins Strt Flush (2 HC)..0.6+
3 Card Ins Strt Flush (1 HC)....0.6+
3 Card Straight Flush (0 HC)....0.6+
4 Card Inside Straight (4 HC)...0.6-
2 Card Royal (KQ,KJ,QJ)........0.6-
2 Card Royal (A high/no 10).....0.5+
4 Card Inside Straight (3 HC)...0.5+
3 High Cards no Ace............0.5+
3 CD Dbl Ins Strt Flush (1 HC)..0.5
2 High Cards...................0.5-
3 CD Inside Strt Flush (0 HC)...0.5-
2 Card Royal (w/10 no Ace)......0.5-
1 High Card....................0.5-
3 CD Dbl Ins Strt Flush (0 HC)..0.4+
RAZGU Draw 5 Cards.............0.4-
```

JB-10   Jacks or Better

PAY TABLE Per Coin; 5 Coin Play	FREQUENCY OF WINNERS
Royal Flush.......800 ...	1/ 40,200
Straight Flush.....50 ...	1/ 9,400
4 of a Kind.(A's).100 ...	1/ 5,200
(Jacks).. 50 ...	1/ 5,200
(Others)..25 ...	1/ 425
Full House.........8 ...	1/ 87
Flush..............5 ...	1/ 92
Straight...........4 ...	1/ 89
Three of a Kind.....3 ...	1/ 14
Two Pairs..........2 ...	1/ 8
Jacks or Better.....1 ...	1/ 5
Non-Winners 55%	

PAYBACK: 99.3%

This game is proprietary to the Golden Nugget downtown in Las Vegas, where it initiated a "payback war" focused on making players aware of the advantages of this casino's high payback video pokers. Until that time, hardly a word was ever mentioned about the liberal paybacks on VP's. One might imagine that the casinos were hoping this dreaded low-vig video game, invented primarily to amuse the timid non-gamblers, would just vanish. That one "shot" opened the floodgates to a torrent of new games and ultimately to a "bonus poker" boom.

"Aces and Jacks" also offers a liberal Sequential Royal bonus which is worth over 0.4% additional in payback.

JB-10 Jacks or Better

```
Royal Flush..................800
Four Aces....................100
Straight Flush...............50
Four J's.....................50
Four of a Kind...............25
4 CD Royal...................18+
Full House...................8
3 of a Kind (Aces)...........7+
3 of a Kind (J's)............5+
Flush........................5
3 of a Kind .................4+
Straight.....................4
4 Card Straight Flush........3.4
Two Pairs....................2.5
4 Card Ins Straight Flush....2+
Pair Aces....................1.7
Pair J's or higher...........1.6
3 Card Royal.................1.5
4 Card Flush.................1+
4 Card Straight (3 Hi Cards)....0.9-
Low Pair (any)...............0.8+
4 Card Straight (2 HC).......0.8+
4 Card Straight (1 HC).......0.7+
3 CD Inside Strt Flush (2 HC)...0.7+
3 Card Straight Flush (1 HC)....0.7+
4 Card Straight (0 HC).......0.7-
3 CD Dbl Ins Strt Flush (2 HC)..0.6+
3 Card Ins Strt Flush (1 HC)....0.6+
3 Card Straight Flush (0 HC)....0.6+
4 Card Inside Straight (4 HC)...0.6-
2 Card Royal (KQ,KJ,QJ)......0.6-
2 Card Royal (A high/no 10)....0.5+
4 Card Inside Strt (3 HC)....0.5+
3 High Cards no Ace..........0.5+
3 CD Dbl Ins Strt Flush (1 HC)..0.5
2 High Cards.................0.5-
3 Card Ins Strt Flush (0 HC)....0.5-
2 Card Royal (w/10 no Ace)...0.5-
1 High Card..................0.5-
4 CD Dbl Ins Strt Flush (0 HC)..0.4+
RAZGU Draw 5 Cards...........0.4-
```

JB-11 Jacks or Better

PAY TABLE Per Coin; 5 Coin Play	FREQUENCY OF WINNERS

```
Royal Flush.....1,000  ...   1/   35,000
(# prime suit). 2,000
Straight Flush.....50  ...   1/    8,700
(# prime suit)....100
4 of a Kind.......25   ...     1/     425
Full House.........8   ...     1/      87
Flush..............5   ...     1/      90
(# prime suit).....10
Straight...........4   ...     1/      90
Three of a Kind.....3  ...     1/      14
Two Pairs..........2   ...     1/       8
Jacks or Better.....1  ...     1/       5
Non-Winners   55%
```

PAYBACK: 99.7%

This game, known as "Bonus Flush", is proprietary to the Golden Nugget downtown in Las Vegas, where it and JB10 initiated a "payback war". The game is extremely popular and always gets billboard ads at the GN. It has been imitated as "Bonus Pay Bonanza" and "Double Pay Diamonds"(no suit choice) in other casinos

Each machine has its designated prime suit, which earns double awards on flushes, straight flushes and royals in suit. Sporting one of the longest pay tables, the glass takes a bit of time to decode. The strategy is complex, requiring a lot of concentration to optimize "in suit" partial flushes.

JB-11 Jacks or Better

```
#Royal Flush................2,000
Royal Flush.................1,000
#Straight Flush..............100
Straight Flush................50
#4 Card Royal.................45-
4 of a Kind...................25
4 Card Royal.................22+
# Flush.......................10
Full House.....................8
#4 Card Straight Flush.........6
Flush..........................5
3 of a Kind...................4+
#4 Card Inside Straight Flush...4+
Straight.......................4
4 Card Straight Flush.........3+
#3 Card Royal Flush...........3-
Two Pairs....................2.5
4 Card Inside Straight Flush....2.2
#4 Card Flush................1.9
3 Card Royal Flush..........1.7
Pair J's or higher..........1.5
#3 Card Straight Flush (1 HC)...1+
4 Card Flush..................1+
#3 CD Ins Strt Flush (2 HC).....1-
#3 CD Straight Flush (0 HC).....0.9
#3 CD Ins Strt Flush (1 HC).....0.9-
#3 CD Dbl Ins Strt Flu(2 HC)....0.9-
4 Card Straight (3 HC).........0.9-
Low Pair.....................0.8+
4 Card Straight (2 HC).........0.8+
#3 Card Ins Strt Flush (0 HC)...0.8-
#3 Card Dbl Ins Strt Flu (1HC)..0.7+
4 Card Straight (1 HC).........0.7+
3 Card Ins Strt Flush (2 HC)....0.7+
#2 Card Royal (KQ,KJ,QJ).......0.7+
#2 Card Royal (A high/ no 10)...0.7+
3 Card Straight Flush (1 HC)....0.7
4 Card Straight (0 HC).........0.7-
#3 CD Dbl Ins Strt Flu (0 HC)...0.6+
3 CD Dbl Ins Strt Flu (2 HC)....0.6
3 CD Inside Strt Flush (1 HC)...0.6
3 CD Strt Flush (0 hi cards)....0.6
#2CD Royal (w/10, no Ace).......0.6
4 CD Inside Straight (4 HC).....0.6-
2 CD Royal (KQ,KJ,QJ),,,,.......0.6-
2 CD Royal (A high/no 10).......0.5+
3 High Cards no Ace...........0.5+
4 Card Inside Strt (3 HC).......0.5+
3 CD Dbl Ins Strt Flush (1 HC)..0.5
2 High Cards..................0.5
3 CD Inside Strt Flush (0 HC)...0.5
2 Card Royal (w/10 no Ace)......0.5-
1 High Card...................0.5-
3 CD Dbl Ins Strt Flush (0 HC)..0.4
RAZGU Draw 5 Cards.............0.4-
```

33

JB-12 Jacks or Better

PAY TABLE Per Coin; 5 Coin Play	FREQUENCY OF WINNERS

```
Sequential AKQJT 48,000    1/ 4,700,000
Royal Flush.......800 ...   1/   40,200
Straight Flush.....50 ...   1/    9,200
4 of a Kind.......25        1/      425
Full House.........8 ...    1/       87
Flush..............5 ...    1/       92
Straight...........4 ...    1/       89
Three of a Kind.....3 ...   1/       14
Two Pairs..........2 ...    1/        8
Jacks or Better.....1 ...   1/        5
Non-Winners  55%
```

PAYBACK: 97.6+%

MegaPoker is the name of Nevada's state-wide quarter game of chance in which several hundred VP's are linked to share a progressive Jackpot for a Sequential Royal. The machines are found in taverns, but not in casinos. The strategy shown corresponds to a Jackpot at $60,000, equivalent to a per-coin payout of 48,000 for 1. This is a typical value. The strategy will increasingly create higher ranking for the partial Royals as the meter increases.

The payback is 97.6% at the initial reset value of $20,000 and increases by about 0.33% for each added $20,000. The Atlantic City casinos offer a radically different game using the same name.

JB-12　Jacks or Better

```
Sequential Royal........48,000
4 Card Sequential Royal...1,020+
Royal Flush...............800
Straight Flush.............50
4 of a Kind................25
3 Card Sequential Royal......23+
4 Card Royal...............18+
Full House..................8
Flush.......................5
3 of a Kind................4+
Straight....................4
4 Card Straight Flush........4-
Two Pairs...................3-
4 Card Inside Strt Flush......2+
Pair J's or higher...........1.5
3 Card Royal................1.5
2 CD Seq. Royal (no Ten)......1.1
4 Card Flush................1+
2 CD Seq. Royal (incl Ten)....1.0
4 Card Straight (3 Hi Cards)..0.9
Low Pair....................0.8+
4 Card Straight (2 HC)........0.8+
4 Card Straight (1 HC)........0.7+
3 CD Ins Strt Flush (2 HC).....0.7+
3 Card Straight Flush (1 HC)...0.7+
4 Card Straight (0 HC).........0.7-
3 CD Dbl Ins Strt Flush(2 HC)..0.6+
3 CD Ins Strt Flush (1 HC).....0.6+
3 Card Straight Flush (0 HC)...0.6+
4 CD Inside Straight (4 HC)....0.6-
2 CD Royal (KQ,KJ,QJ)..........0.6-
2 CD Royal (Ace High/no 10)....0.5+
4 Card Inside Straight (3 HC)..0.5+
3 High Cards (No Ace).........0.5+
3 CD Dbl Ins Strt Flush(1 HC)..0.5
2 High Cards.................0.5-
3 CD Ins Strt Flush (0 HC).....0.5-
2 Card Royal (w/10 no Ace).....0.5-
1 High Card..................0.5-
3 CD Dbl Ins Str Flush (0 HC)..0.4+
RAZGU Draw 5 Cards...........0.4-
```

JB-13   Jacks or Better

PAY TABLE Per Coin; 5 Coin Play	FREQUENCY OF WINNERS

```
Seq.In Suit TJQKA 400,000    1/ 18,700,000
Seq. (Out Suit)     4,000    1/ 6,300,000
Royal Flush.......800 ...       1/   40,000
Straight Flush....100 ...       1/    8,000
4 of a Kind.Aces..160 ...       1/    5,000
          2-3-4s...80 ...       1/    1,900
          5 - K's..50 ...       1/      600
Full House.........8 ...          1/     95
Flush..............6 ...          1/     90
Straight...........4 ...          1/     80
Three of a Kind....3 ...          1/     13
Two Pairs..........1 ...          1/      8
Jacks or Better....1 ...          1/      5
Non-Winners   55%
```

PAYBACK: 95.8+%

POKERMANIA is the name of this super-progressive game which links machines all over Atlantic City in a race for a Sequential Royal in a specific suit which is assigned to each machine. Our strategy table shows three values of the big meter (100K, 300K and 500K) and the consolation meters (1K, 3K and 5K) in dollars. These are typically in the expected range. This game offers a 95.8% payback at minimum reset values on the meters and an additional 0.5% for each 100K dollars on the major Jackpot. With a lifestyle-changing jackpot, it's for a special kind of player known as a dreamer (with deep pockets).

JB-13 Jacks or Better

Meters in Dollars---->>	100K 1K	300K 3K	500K 5K
* Sequential Royal in Suit...80,000		240,000	400,000
* 4-Card Seq. Royal In Suit...1,700		5,100	8,500
* Seq. Royal (Not in Suit)......800		2,400	4,000
Royal Flush (Not in Seq.).....800			
Four Aces....................160			
Straight Flush...............100			
Four 2-3-4's..................80			
Four 5-Kings..................50			
* 3 Card Seq. Royal in Suit......38		112	186
* 4 Cd Seq. Royal non-suit.......19		54	86
4 Card Royal (non-seq)........ 19			
Three Aces................... 10			
Full House.. 8			
Three 2-3-4s...................6.6			
Flush..........................6			
4 Card Straight Flush..........5.7			
Three of a Kind (5-K's)........5.3			
Straight.....................4			
4 Card Inside Strt. Flush......3.4			
Pair ACES....................1.7			
Two Pairs (Bar Aces)...........1.6			
* 3 Cd Seq. Royal Non-Suit.......1.5		2.2	2.9
3 Card Royal non-seq...........1.5			
High Pair (J-Q-K's).............1.4			
* 2 Cd Seq. Royal In Suit........1.3		3.0	4.7
4 Card Flush..................1.2			
4 Card Straight (3 HC).........0.9-			
3 Card Strt. Flush (1 HC)......0.8+			
3 Card Ins Strt Flush (2 HC)...0.8			
Pair 2-3-4's..................0.8			
4 Card Straight (2 HC).........0.8			
3 Card Strt. Flush (0 HC)......0.7+			
4 Card Straight (1HC)..........0.7+			
Low Pair (5-10's)..............0.7+			
3 Card Ins Strt Flush (1HC).....0.7			
4 Card Straight (no HC)........0.7-			
3 Cd Dbl Ins Strt Flush (2HC).. 0.6+			
* 2 Cd Seq. Royal (Bar A-10)......0.6		0.62	0.63
3 Card Ins Strt Flush (0 HC)....0.6			
4 Cd Inside Straight (4HC)......0.6-			
2 Card Royal (KQ,KJ,QJ only) .. 0.6-			
2 Card Royal (AK,AQ,AJ only)....0.6-			
3 Cd Dbl Ins Strt Flush (1HC).. 0.5+			
4 Cd Inside Straight (3HC)......0.5+			
Three High cards (KQJ).........0.5			
* 1 Cd Seq. Royal in Suit X10... 0.5+		0.5+	0.6-
3 Cd Dbl Ins Strt Flush (0HC).. 0.5-			
Two High Cards................0.4+			
2 Card Royal (K-10,Q-10,J-10).. 0.4+			
One High Card.................0.4+			
* 2 Cd Seq.Royal (A-10;non-suit)..0.4		0.5-	0.5
* TEN in Sequence and Suit........0.3+		0.4	0.4+
RAZGU None of Above Draw 5.....0.3			

37

JB-14   Jacks or Better

PAY TABLE Per Coin; 4 Coin Play	FREQUENCY OF WINNERS

```
Royal Flush.......500 ...   1/   51,800
Straight Flush....100 ...   1/    7,500
4 of a Kind.......25         1/      440
Full House........10 ...     1/       90
Flush..............8 ...     1/       60
Straight...........6 ...     1/       60
Three of a Kind....3 ...     1/       14
Two Pairs..........1 ...     1/        8
Jacks or Better....1 ...     2/       11
Non-Winners  58%
```

PAYBACK: 94.0 %

This game is on the Player's Choice multi-game terminals in race tracks and truck stops in Louisiana and other states which have fostered the marriage of "GG's and VP's". In the Bayou State there is a 94% cap on payback and also a limit of $500 on the maximum award. The latter makes it adviseable never to play at over 4 coins, even though the machine may take up to 8 coins. Obviously, the players have had very little say in the matter of what's available.

To make matters worse, the pay table causes the strategy to become long and complex with many "poor" hands being playable, e.g., 2 card straight flushes and 3 card straights, all peculiar to this machine, not most other VP's.

JB-14 Jacks or Better

```
Royal Flush.................500
Straight Flush..............100
4 of a Kind.................25
4 Card Royal................12+
Full House..................10
Flush.......................8
4 Card Straight Flush.......6+
Straight....................6
3 of a Kind.................4+
4 Card Inside Straight Flush...4-
Two Pairs...................2-
4 Card Flush................1.6
3 Card Royal................1.4
Pair J's or higher..........1.4
4 CD Straight (3 Hi Cards)....1.2
4 CD Straight (2 Hi Cards)....1.2
4 CD Straight (1 Hi Card)....1.1
4 CD Straight (0 Hi Cards)....1+
3 Card Straight Flush (1 HC)...1-
3 CD Inside Strt Flush (2 HC)..0.9+
3 Card Straight Flush (0 HC)...0.9+
3 Card Ins Strt Flush (1 HC)...0.8+
4 Card Inside Straight (4 HC)..0.8-
3 CD Dbl Ins Strt Flush (2 HC).0.8-
3 CD Inside Strt Flush (0 HC)..0.7+
4 CD Inside Strt (3 HC).......0.7
Low Pair....................0.7-
3 CD Dbl Ins Strt Flush (1 HC).0.7-
4 Card Inside Strt (2 HC)....0.6+
2 Card Royal (KQ,KJ,QJ).......0.6
3 Card Flush (2 High Cards)...0.6
3 CD Dbl Ins Str Flush (0 HC)..0.6-
4 Card Inside Strt (1 HC)....0.6-
2 Card Royal (A high/no 10)...0.5+
3 High Cards no Ace..........0.5+
4 Card Inside Straight (0 HC)..0.5+
3 Card Flush.(1 High Card)....0.5
2 High Cards................0.5-
2 Card Royal (w/10 no Ace)....0.5-
1 High Card.................0.4+
3 Card Flush (0 High Cards)...0.4
2 Card Straight Flush.........0.3+
3 Card Straight.............0.3+
RAZGU Draw 5 Cards..........0.3
```

PAY TABLE Per Coin; 5 Coin Play	FREQUENCY OF WINNERS

```
Royal Flush.......800 ...   1/  42,800
Straight Flush.....50 ...   1/   9,200
4 Aces + a Face...320 ...   1/  18,000
4 Aces...........160 ...    1/   6,000
4 K-Q-J + A,K,Q or J..160 ...  1/   6,900
4 K-Q-J's..........80 ...    1/   2,300
4 Twos- Tens.......50 ...    1/    650
Full House........10 ...     1/     90
Flush..............6 ...     1/     90
Straight...........4 ...     1/     80
Three of a Kind.....3 ...    1/     13
Two Pairs..........1 ...     1/      8
Jacks or Better.....1 ...    1/      5
Non-Winners  55%
```

PAYBACK: 100.3 %

This game (called Double Double Jackpot by Sigma) is the most liberal of the "double double" entries but suffers from being available only in dollar machines and from paying only 1,600 on its mini-jackpot, whereas others pay 2,000. It's a mystery why players would sacrifice 1.5% in payback for that slight bit of "pie in the sky". In quarter machines the 10 / 4 becomes 8 / 5, dropping the payback to 99.6%.

The two "info" lines in the strategy are to remind players that we don't hold the kicker if dealt triplets A/K/Q/ or J's.

JB-15   Jacks or Better

```
Royal Flush..................800
Four ACES + Face.............320
Four ACES....................200+
4 FACES + Ace/Face...........160
Four FACES...................100+
Straight Flush...............50
Four 2-10's..................50
4 Card Royal ................19
Three ACES...................12
3 Aces + Face...........10+ info
Full House...................10
Three FACES..................8.5
3 Faces + Ace/Face.......6.7 info
Flush........................6
Three 2-10's.................5.4
Straight.....................4
4 Card Straight Flush........3.8
4 Card Inside Straight Flush...2.5
Pair ACES....................1.9
Two Pairs....................1.8
Pair FACES...................1.5
3 Card Royal.................1.4
4 Card Flush.................1.3
4 Card Straight (3 HC).......0.9
4 Card Straight (2 HC).......0.8
Pair 2-Tens..................0.7+
4 Card Straight (1 HC).......0.7
3 Card Straight Flush (1 HC)...0.7
4 Card Straight (0 HC).......0.7
3 CD Dbl Ins Strt Flush (2 HC).0.6
3 Card Straight Flush (0 HC)...0.6
3 CD Inside Strt Flush (1 HC)..0.6
4 Card Inside Strt (4 HC)......0.6
2 Card Royal (No 10).........0.5
4 Card Inside Straight (3 HC)..0.5
3 CD Dbl Ins Strt Flush (1 HC).0.5
3 Card Ins Strt Flush (0 HC)...0.5
3 High Cards KQJ.............0.5
Two High Cards...............0.4+
2 Card Royal (K/Q/J-10)......0.4+
One High Card................0.4
3 CD Dbl Ins Strt Flush (0 HC).0.4
RAZGU (DRAW 5)...............0.3
```

PAY TABLE Per Coin; 5 Coin Play	FREQUENCY OF WINNERS

```
Royal Flush.......800 ...   1/  40,200
LO Royal 2-6......800       1/ 160,000
Straight Flush.....50 ...   1/   9,200
4 of a Kind.......40 ...    1/     425
Full House.........6 ...    1/      87
Flush..............5 ...    1/      91
Straight...........4 ...    1/      89
Three of a Kind.....3 ...   1/      14
Two Pairs..........2 ...    1/       8
Jacks or Better.....1 ...   1/       5
Non-Winners  55%
```

PAYBACK: 99.8 %

This game (called Hi-Low Royal) is seldom found any more in a dedicated machine, but is making a big comeback on the multi-game touch screen machines. The key payout is the 40 for 1 on Quads, with some paying only 35 or even less. The strateegy is fairly easy to master since the partial "LO royals" show up in only 3 places in the ranking table.

The Royals (high and low) make up 2.5% of the payback and the Quads make up 10%. One can see that any session in which the quads take a vacation will necessarily be tough and brief, especially since 5-coin play is mandatory to get the 800 on either high or low Royals.

JB-16   Jacks or Better

```
Royal Flush.................800
Lo-Royal (2-thru-6).........800
Straight Flush..............50
4 of a Kind.................40
4 Card LO-Royal.............19+
4 Card Royal................18+
Full House...................6
Flush........................5
3 of a Kind.................4+
Straight.....................4
4 Card Straight Flush.......3+
Two Pairs...................2+
4 Card Inside Strt Flush....2+
Pair J's or higher..........1.5
3 Card Royal................1.5
3 Card LO-Royal.............1.2
4 Card Flush................1.1
4 Card Straight (3 Hi Cards)...1.0-
Low Pair......... ..........0.8+
4 Card Straight (2 HC).........0.8+
4 Card Straight (1 HC).........0.7+
3 Card Ins Strt Flush (2 HC)...0.7+
3 CD Straight Flush (1 HC).....0.7+
4 Card Straight (0 HC).........0.7-
3 CD Dbl Ins Strt Flush(2 HC)..0.6+
3 CD Ins Strt Flush (1 HC).....0.6+
3 Card Straight Flush (0 HC)...0.6+
2 Card Royal (KQ, KJ, QJ)......0.6+
4 CD Inside Straight (4 HC)....0.6-
2 Card Royal (A high/no 10)....0.6-
4 Card Inside Straight (3 HC)..0.5+
3 High Cards no Ace............0.5+
3 Card Ins Strt Flush (0 HC)...0.5+
3 CD Dbl Ins Strt Flush (1 HC).0.5+
2 High Cards...................0.5-
2 Card Royal (w/10 no Ace).....0.5-
1 High Card....................0.5-
3 CD Dbl Ins Str Flush (0 HC)..0.4+
2 Card LO-Royal 4-5, 5-6.......0.4-
RAZGU Draw 5 Cards.............0.3+
```

43

JB-17 Jacks or Better

| PAY TABLE | | | FREQUENCY |
Per Coin; 5 Coin Play			OF WINNERS
Royal Flush.......800	...	1/	40,500
Straight Flush.....50	...	1/	9,200
4 of a Kind. (Aces) 80	...	1/	5,100
(Kings) 60		1/	5,100
(Queens) 40		1/	5,100
(2-Jacks) 20		1/	550
Full House..........8	...	1/	87
Flush...............6	...	1/	91
Straight............4	...	1/	89
Three of a Kind.....3	...	1/	14
Two Pairs...........2	...	1/	8
Jacks or Better.....1	...	2/	9
Non-Winners 55%			

PAYBACK: 99.6 %

This was an early try at a "bonus poker" in a game which was proprietary to Circus and exclusive to their smoke-free Silver City property (now full of smoke). Known as "Fours Plus", this full-pay game is making a comeback on the multi-game touch-screen machines since there seems to be dearth of good games to fill them up. The cut of one unit on the Full House is balanced off by the premium Quads.

Note that the choice between a 3-Card Royal and a High Pair depends on whether the pair is Jacks or a higher pair.

44

JB-17　Jacks or Better

```
Royal Flush.................800
Straight Flush...............50
4 of a Kind (Aces)...........80
           (Kings)..........60
           (Queens).........40
4 of a Kind................ .20
4 Card Royal................18+
Full House...................8
Flush........................6
3 of a Kind.................4+
Straight.....................4
4 Card Straight Flush.........3+
Two Pairs....................2.5
4 Card Inside Strt Flush.......2.3
Pair Aces....................1.7
Pair Kings...................1.6
Pair Queens..................1.6-
3 Card Royal.................1.5+
Pair J's ....................1.5
4 Card Flush.................1.2
4 Card Straight (3 Hi Cards)...0.9-
4 Card Straight (2 HC).........0.8+
Low Pair.....................0.8
4 Card Straight (1 HC).........0.7+
3 CD Inside Strt Flush (2 HC)..0.7+
3 Card Straight Flush (1 HC)...0.7+
4 Card Straight (0 HC).........0.7-
3 CD Dbl Ins Strt Flush (2 HC).0.6+
3 Card Ins Strt Flush (1 HC)...0.6+
3 Card Straight Flush (0 HC)...0.6+
2 Card Royal (KQ, KJ, QJ),.....0.6+
4 Card Inside Straight (4 HC)..0.6
2 Card Royal (A high/no 10)....0.6-
3 CD Inside Strt Flush (0 HC)..0.5+
3 CD Dbl Ins Strt Flush (1 HC).0.5+
4 CD Inside Straight (3 HC)....0.5+
3 High Cards no Ace...........0.5+
2 High Cards.................0.5
2 CD Royal (w/10 no Ace).......0.5-
1 High Card..................0.5-
3 CD Dbl Ins Strt Flush (0 HC).0.4+
RAZGU Draw 5 Cards.............0.3+
```

PAY TABLE Per Coin; 5 Coin Play		FREQUENCY OF WINNERS	
Royal Flush.......800 ...		1/	39,800
Straight Flush....100 ...		1/	8,300
4 of a Kind.(Aces) 50 ...		1/	5,100
(2-3-4's) 40		1/	5,100
(5-Kings) 20		1/	550
Full House.........8 ...		1/	87
Flush..............5 ...		1/	91
Straight...........4 ...		1/	90
Three of a Kind.....3 ...		1/	14
Two Pairs..........2 ...		1/	8
Jacks or Better.....1 ...		1/	5
Non-Winners 55%			

PAYBACK: 98.3 %

This is the recent Atlantic City translation of the popular Las Vegas game called Bonus Poker, a game which went on to become a classic. It marked a turning point for the better paybacks which followed. the concept of rewarding Quads at various levels found a profoundly receptive audience, willing to accept an 8 / 5 schedule for the enhancement since Quads show up 100 times more often than those elusive Royals.

Note that the lowest Quad rung pays 20, rather than the 25 offered on "full-pay" Bonus Pokers (JB-06), giving the player an extra strategy decision vis-a-vis the 3 Card Royal. That's a small price to pay for a better return.

JB-18   Jacks or Better

```
Royal Flush.................800
Straight Flush..............100
4 of a Kind (Aces)...........50
4 of a Kind (2,3,4s).........40
4 of a Kind.................20
4 Card Royal................18+
Full House...................8
4 Card Straight Flush.........5.5
Three of a Kind (Aces)........5.3
Flush.........................5
3 of a Kind.................5-
Straight.....................4
4 Card Inside Strt Flush......3.2
Two Pairs....................2.5
Pair Aces....................1.6
3 Card Royal (No Ace).........1.5+
Pair J's ....................1.5+
3 Card Royal (w/ Ace).........1.5
4 Card Flush.................1.2
4 Card Straight (3 Hi Cards)...0.9-
Low Pair (2-3-4)..............0.8+
3 Card Straight Flush (1 HC)...0.8+
4 Card Straight (2 HC)........0.8+
Low Pair (5 to 10)............0.8
3 Card Ins Strt Flush (2 HC)...0.8-
4 Card Straight (1 HC)........0.7+
3 Card Straight Flush (0 HC)...0.7
3 Card Ins Strt Flush (1 HC)...0.7-
4 Card Straight (0 HC)........0.7-
3 CD Dbl Ins Strt Flu (2 HC)...0.6+
2 Card Royal (KQ, KJ, QJ),.....0.6
4 Card Ins Straight (4 HC).....0.6-
3 CD Inside Strt Flush (0 HC)..0.6-
2 Card Royal (A high/no 10)....0.6-
3 CD Dbl Ins Strt Flush (1 HC).0.5+
4 Card Ins Straight (3 HC).....0.5+
3 High Cards (No Ace).........0.5+
2 High Cards.................0.5-
2 Card Royal (w/10 no Ace).....0.5-
1 High Card.................0.5-
3 CD Dbl Ins Strt Flush (0 HC).0.4+
RAZGU Draw 5 Cards............0.3+
```

47

PAY TABLE Per Coin; 5 Coin Play		FREQUENCY OF WINNERS	
Royal Flush.......	800 ...	1/	39,800
Straight Flush.....	50 ...	1/	8,300
4 of a Kind.(TWOs)	50 ...	1/	5,100
(3-4-5's)	40	1/	5,100
(6-Kings)	25	1/	550
Full House.........	6 ...	1/	87
Flush..............	5 ...	1/	91
Straight...........	4 ...	1/	90
Three of a Kind.....	3 ...	1/	14
Two Pairs..........	2 ...	1/	8
Jacks or Better.....	1 ...	1/	5
Non-Winners 55%			

PAYBACK: 96.8 %

This is the earliest Atlantic City entry, a corruption of the popular game Las Vegas game called Bonus Poker, a game which went on to become a classic. However, at the time it marked an important turning point for the better paybacks which followed, cracking the 96% sound barrier. Since it was equal in payback and easier to learn, this game probably reversed the "joker poker" craze that was the hallmark of A.C. games since casinos were approved in 1978.

More liberal versions paying 7 / 5 are also available now in A.C. and virtually all other locales. This strategy is very closely applicable to those also.

JB-19   Jacks or Better

```
Royal Flush................800
Straight Flush...............50
4 of a Kind (Twos)...........80
           (3,4,5s)..........40
4 of a Kind (6-A).............25
4 Card Royal..................18+
3 of a Kind (Twos).............6.5
Full House.....................6
Flush..........................5
3 of a Kind  (3,4,5's).........4.7
3 of a Kind  (6-Ace)...........4.1
Straight.......................4
4 Card Straight Flush..........3.4
Two Pairs......................2.3
4 Card Inside Strt Flush.......2.2
High Pair (J-Q-K-A)............1.5+
3 Card Royal...................1.5-
4 Card Flush...................1.2
Pair (Twos)....................0.9+
4 Card Straight (3 Hi Cards)....0.9-
Low Pair (3-4-5's).............0.8+
Low Pair (6-10's)..............0.8+
4 Card Straight (2 HC).........0.8
4 Card Straight (1 HC).........0.7+
3 Card Ins Strt Flush (2 HC)....0.7
3 Card Straight Flush (1 HC)....0.7
4 Card Straight (0 HC).........0.7-
3 CD Dbl Ins Strt Flush (2 HC)..0.6+
4 Card Inside Straight (4 HC)...0.6
3 Card Ins Strt Flush (1 HC)....0.6
3 Card Straight Flush (0 HC)....0.6
2 Card Royal (KQ, KJ, QJ),......0.6
2 Card Royal (A high/no 10).....0.6
4 Card Inside Straight (3 HC)...0.5+
3 High Cards no Ace............0.5+
3 CD Dbl Ins Strt Flush (1 HC)..0.5
3 Card Ins Strt Flush (0 HC)....0.5+
2 High Cards...................0.5-
2 Card Royal (w/10 no Ace)......0.5-
1 High Card....................0.5-
3 CD Dbl Ins Strt Flush (0 HC)..0.4
RAZGU Draw 5 Cards.............0.3+
```

JB-20   Jacks or Better

PAY TABLE Per Coin; 5 Coin Play		FREQUENCY OF WINNERS	
Royal Flush.......800 ...		1/	43,500
Straight Flush....200 ...		1/	7,100
4 of a Kind....... 40 ...		1/	445
Full House..........8 ...		1/	92
Flush...............8 ...		1/	64
Straight............8 ...		1/	55
Three of a Kind.....3 ...		1/	15
Two Pairs...........1 ...		1/	8
Jacks or Better.....1 ...		2/	11
Non-Winners 55%			

PAYBACK: 100.7 %

Known as "All American Poker", this extremely liberal game survives because very few people have learned its lengthy strategy well enough to matter. Those who have are thriving on it, since the few machines found around are always available. It is also offered (same name) in a 30 on Quads version which falls a tad short of 100% payback.

On most machines, the frequency of winners among the Full House, Flush and Straight categories are nearly equal although the pay lines are quite different. Here, the equal pay lines create a dispersion in those frequencies.

For the astute and patient players who don't mind isolation from the crowd, this is the best game around.

JB-20 Jacks or Better

```
Royal Flush.................800
Straight Flush..............200
4 of a Kind.................40
4 Card Royal................19+
4 Card Straight Flush.......10+
Full House..................8
Flush.......................8
Straight....................8
4 Card Inside Strt Flush....6.1
3 of a Kind.................4.9
3 Card Royal (K,Q High).....1.8
Two Pairs...................1.6
4 Card Flush................1.6
3 Card Royal Ace High.......1.6-
4 Card Straight (1,2,3 HC)..1.5
Pair J's or higher..........1.4
4 Card Straight (0 HC)......1.4-
3 Card Strt Flush (1 Hi Card)..1.4-
3 Card Straight Flush (0 HC)...1.3-
3 CD Ins.Strt Flush (1,2 HC)...1.1-
3 CD Ins Strt Flush (0 HC).....1.0-
4 CD Inside Straight (4 HC)....0.9-
3 CD Dbl Ins Strt Flush (2 HC).0.9-
4 Card Inside Strt (3 HC)......0.9-
4 Card Ins.Strt (2 Hi Cards)...0.8+
3 CD Dbl Ins Strt Flush (1 HC).0.8-
4 Card Inside Straight (1 HC)..0.7+
Low Pair....................0.7
3 CD Dbl Ins Strt Flu (0 HC)...0.7-
4 Card Inside Straight.........0.7-
3 Card Straight (Q-J-10).......0.6+
2 Card Royal (KQ,KJ,QJ)........0.6+
3 High Cards no Ace............0.6+
3 Card Flush (2 HC)............0.6
2 Card Royal (A high/no 10)....0.6-
2 Card Royal (w/10 no Ace).....0.5+
3 Card Straight (9-10-J).......0.5+
3 Card Flush (1 HC)............0.5
3 High Cards (AKQ only)........0.5
2 High Cards................0.5-
2 Card Royal (Ace-10).........0.4+
1 High Card.................0.4+
3 Card Straight.............0.4+
3 Card Flush................0.4-
2 Card Straight Flush.........0.4-
2 CD Inside Straight Flush....0.4-
RAZGU Draw 5 Cards............0.3+
```

51

PAY TABLE Per Coin; 5 Coin Play	FREQUENCY OF WINNERS
Royal Flush.......800 ...	1/ 48,000
Straight Flush.... 50 ...	1/ 8,800
4 of a Kind(Aces) 160 ...	1/ 5,000
(2-3-4) 80 ...	1/ 1,900
(5-Kings) 50 ...	1/ 600
Full House........10 ...	1/ 90
Flush..............7 ...	1/ 70
Straight...........5 ...	1/ 70
Three of a Kind.....3 ...	1/ 14
Two Pairs..........1 ...	1/ 8
Jacks or Better.....1 ...	1/ 5
Non-Winners 55%	

(left margin, handwritten: 10/7 Double Bonus)

PAYBACK: 100.1 %

Double Bonus Poker is well on its way to becoming a classic as evidenced by the arrival of a number of lower-paying imitators, the most insidious of which is the 9 / 6 version, designed to capitalize on the reputation of a standard full-pay Jacks (JB-01). One glance at the lengthy strategy table tells the story--it plays much differently!

Along with Flush Attack, this game was an early purveyor of the "push on Two Pairs" in order to fatten up the Quads awards. When one considers that it takes triplets to produce a net winner (without a wild card), the raw truth, its mean and streaky nature is apparent. But it pays well and its offspring are even meaner.

JB-21   Jacks or Better

```
Royal Flush.................800
Four ACES...................160
Four 2-3-4's................80
Straight Flush..............50
Four 5-K's..................50
4 Card Royal................19
Three ACES..................10+
Full House..................10
Flush.......................7
Three 2-3-4's...............7-
Three 5-K's.................5+
Straight....................5
4 Card Straight Flush.......4-
4 Card Inside Strt Flush....3-
Two Pairs...................1.8
Pair ACES...................1.8-
3 Card Royal (KQJ / QJT)....1.6-
4 Card Flush w/ 3 HCds......1.5+
3 Card Royal (Ace High No 10)..1.5
4 Card Flush (2 HC).........1.5-
Pair K-Q-J's................1.4+
4 Card Flush (0,1 HC).......1.4
3 Card Royal................1.4-
4 Card Straight (0-3 HC)....1+
Pair 2-3-4's................0.8+
3 CD Straigt Flush (1 HC)...0.8-
3 CD Ins. Strt. Flush (2 HC)...0.8-
Pair 5's-10's...............0.7+
3 Card Straight Flush (0 HC)...0.7
3 CD Inside Strt. Flush (1 HC).0.7
4 CD Inside Straight (4 HCd)...0.7-
3 CD Dbl Ins Strt Flush (2 HC).0.7-
4 CD Inside Straight (3 HC)....0.6+
3 Card Ins Strt. Flush (0 HC)..0.6-
2 Card Royal (No A,10)......0.6-
3 CD Dbl Ins. St. Flush (1 HC).0.6-
3 Card Flush w/ AK,AQ,AJ....0.6-
2 Card Royal w/ Ace no 10...0.6-
4 Card Inside Straight (2 HC)..0.5+
Three High Cards KQJ........0.5+
2 Card Royal J-10...........0.5
4 CD Inside Straight (1 HC)....0.5-
3 Card Straight (2 HC)......0.5-
2 Card Royal K or Q/10......0.5-
3 CD Dbl Ins Strt Flush (0 HC).0.5-
Two High Cards..............0.4+
3 Card Flush (1 HC).........0.4+
One High Card...............0.4+
4 CD Inside Straight (0 HC)....0.4+
3 Card Flush (0 HC).........0.4-
RAZGU Draw 5................0.3+
```

53

JB-22   Jacks or Better

<table>
<tr><th colspan="2">PAY TABLE
Per Coin; 5 Coin Play</th><th colspan="2">FREQUENCY
OF WINNERS</th></tr>
<tr><td>Royal Flush.......</td><td>800</td><td>...</td><td>1/ 40,000</td></tr>
<tr><td>Straight Flush....</td><td>50</td><td>...</td><td>1/ 9,500</td></tr>
<tr><td>4 of a Kind (Aces)</td><td>80#</td><td>...</td><td>1/ 5,100</td></tr>
<tr><td>(K-Q-J)</td><td>40*</td><td>...</td><td>1/ 1,700</td></tr>
<tr><td>(5-Kings)</td><td>20</td><td>...</td><td>1/ 630</td></tr>
<tr><td>Full House........</td><td>8</td><td>...</td><td>1/ 90</td></tr>
<tr><td>Flush.............</td><td>5</td><td>...</td><td>1/ 90</td></tr>
<tr><td>Straight..........</td><td>4</td><td>...</td><td>1/ 90</td></tr>
<tr><td>Three of a Kind...</td><td>3</td><td>...</td><td>1/ 14</td></tr>
<tr><td>Two Pairs.........</td><td>2</td><td>...</td><td>1/ 8</td></tr>
<tr><td>Jacks or Better...</td><td>1</td><td>...</td><td>1/ 5</td></tr>
<tr><td>Non-Winners 55%</td><td></td><td></td><td></td></tr>
</table>

PAYBACK: 99.4 %

Double Bonus Jackpot might be termed a "shy" video poker because it sits quietly in the casinos without making a fuss, while its high payback goes virtually unrecognized. All the doubling features are virtually invisible on its glass, written in such small print that even the slot people can't tell you the story, i.e., # means doubled if with a Face card; * means doubled with an Ace or Face. In effect, these pay lines are really 100 and 50 respectively.

That's pretty competitive for an 8 / 5 machine, bringing it almost up to full-pay status, with the added kick of a $100 payout on 4 Aces from a quarter machine. This game should sue the case designer for non-support.

```
Royal Flush.................800
Four ACES + Face............160
Four ACES..................100+
Four FACES + Ace............80
Four FACES..................50+
Straight Flush..............50
Four 2-10's.................20
4 Card Royal................18+
Full House...................8
Three ACES...................7+
Three FACES..................5+
Flush........................5
Three 2-10's.................4+
Straight.....................4
4 Card Straight Flush........3+
Two Pairs...................2.5
4 Card Inside Strt Flush....2.2
Pair ACES...................1.7
Pair FACES..................1.6
3 Card Royal................1.5
4 Card Flush................1.1
4 Card Straight (2,3 HC)....0.9-
Pair 2's-Tens...............0.8
4 Card Straight (1 HC)......0.7+
3 Card Straight Flush (1HC).0.7
4 Card Straight (0 HC)......0.7-
3 Card Ins trt Flush (2 HC).0.6+
3 Card Straight Flush (0 HC).0.6
3 CD Inside Strt Flush (1 HC).0.6
3 CD Dbl Ins Strt Flush (2 HC).0.6
4 Card Inside Straight (4 HC).0.6
2 Card Royal (No 10)........0.6-
4 CD Inside Straight (3 HC).0.5+
Three High Cards KQJ........0.5+
3 CD Dbl Ins Strt Flush (1 HC.0.5
3 Card Ins Strt Flush (0 HC).0.5
Two High Cards..............0.5-
2 Card Royal (K/Q/J-10).....0.5-
One High Card...............0.5-
3 CD Dbl Ins Strt Flush (0 HC).0.4+
RAZGU Draw 5 Cards..........0.3+
```

JB-23   Jacks or Better

PAY TABLE	FREQUENCY
Per Coin; 5 Coin Play	OF WINNERS

```
Royal Flush.......800  ...   1/  46,500
Straight Flush....100  ...   1/   7,400
4 of a Kind (Aces)200  ...   1/   4,400
          (2 - K)  25  ...   1/     480
Full House........10  ...   1/      95
Flush..............8  ...   1/      60
Straight...........5  ...   1/      70
3 of a Kind.(Aces)..6  ...   1/     125
          (2 - K)...3  ...   1/      15
Two Pairs..........1  ...   2/      17
Jacks or Better.....1  ...   1/       5
Non-Winners  53%
```

PAYBACK: 98.8 %

"Nevada Bonus Poker" is one of the more liberal games available in both nickel and quarter multi-game machines. Its Ace-leaning pay table, paying 6 for Three Aces dictates very careful handling of the pre-draw hands with Ace(s). We don't hold A-X (unmatched) or even A-10 (matched) so that we can optimize our chances. Note also that Aces-full are played for the shot at Quad Aces

The premium payouts on Straights, Flushes and Full Houses create many new "playable" hands such as inside straights and 3 card flushes while elevating many 4 card flushes well above 3 card Royals in ranking. This raises the hit frequency (47%) a bit, while challenging our expertise.

JB-23   Jacks or Better

```
Royal Flush................... 800
Four Aces..................... 200
Straight Flush................ 100
Four of a Kind................ 25
4 Card Royal Flush............ 19-
3 Aces........................ 14+
Full House.................... 10
Flush......................... 8
4 Card Straight Flush......... 6+
Straight...................... 5
3 of a Kind................... 4+
4 Card Inside Straight Flush.. 4-
Pair Aces..................... 2+
Two Pairs..................... 1.8
4 Card Flush (2,3 HC)......... 1.7-
3 Card Royal (K or Q high).... 1.6
4 Card Flush.................. 1.5+
3 Card Royal (A high)......... 1.5
High Pair (J-K)............... 1.4
4 Card Straight (2,3 HC)...... 1
3 Card Straight Flush (1 HC).. 1-
3 Card Ins Strt Flush (2 HC).. 0.9+
4 Card Straight (1 HC)........ 0.9
3 Card Straight Flush (0 HC).. 0.9-
4 Card Straight (0 HC)........ 0.8+
3 Card Ins Strt Flush (1 HC).. 0.8
3 CD Dbl Ins Strt Flush (2 HC) 0.7+
4 Card Inside Straight (4 HC). 0.7
Low Pair...................... 0.7-
3 CD Dbl Ins Strt Flush (1 HC) 0.7-
3 Card Ins Strt Flush (0 HC).. 0.6+
4 CD Inside Strt (3 HC)....... 0.6+
2 Card Royal (No 10).......... 0.6
3 CD Dbl Ins Strt Flush (0 HC) 0.6-
4 Card Inside Straight (2 HC). 0.6-
3 High Cards (No Ace)......... 0.5+
Ace........................... 0.5+
3 Card Flush (1 HC)........... 0.5
4 Card Inside Straight (1 HC). 0.5-
2 Card Royal (w/10 no Ace).... 0.5-
Two High Cards (No Ace)....... 0.4+
One High Card................. 0.4+
4 Card Inside Straight (0 HC). 0.4
3 Card Flush (0 HC)........... 0.4
RAZGU (Draw 5 Cards).......... 0.3+
```

PAY TABLE Per Coin; 5 Coin Play	FREQUENCY OF WINNERS

```
Royal Flush.......800 ...    1/   46,500
Straight Flush....100 ...    1/    7,600
4 of a Kind (Aces)200 ...    1/    5,000
          (2-3-4's) 40 ...    1/    2,000
            (5 - K) 25 ...    1/      550
Full House........12 ...     1/       90
Flush..............8 ...     1/       60
Straight...........5 ...     1/       70
3 of a Kind........3 ...     1/       14
Two Pairs..........1 ...     1/        8
Jacks or Better.....1 ...    1/        5
Non-Winners  53%
```

PAYBACK: 99.3 %

"Power House Poker" is another "bonus poker"variation combining some "double bonus" features (200 on Quad Aces and a 12/ 8 Full House/ Flush schedule) with its inherent drawbacks (push on Two Pairs). What results from this blend is a medium payback, extremely streaky adventure. Generally available in slant-tops for quarters.

While not as difficult as JB-23 to master, this game still has a very complex strategy table laced with some three card flushes and inside straights to contend with. Note that we would hold only the Ace when dealt it with an (suit) unmatched face card. Also, that we keep both pairs in Two Pair with Aces and stand on Aces Full Houses.

JB-24   Jacks or Better

```
Royal Flush................... 800
Four Aces..................... 200
Straight Flush............... 100
4 of a Kind (2,3,4)........... 40
4 of a Kind   (5-K)........... 25
4 Card Royal Flush........... 18+
Full House.................... 12
3 Aces....................... 12-
Flush.......................... 8
4 Card Straight Flush......... 6+
3 of a Kind (2,3,4)........... 5+
Straight....................... 5
3 of a Kind (5-King).......... 4+
4 Card Inside Straight Flush.. 4-
Two Pairs.................... 1.9
Pair Aces................... 1.9-
4 Card Flush (2,3 HC)....... 1.7
3 Card Royal (K,Q high)..... 1.6+
4 Card Flush................ 1.6
3 Card Royal (A high)....... 1.5
High Pair (J-K)............. 1.4
4 Card Straight (2,3 HC).... 1.0
3 Card Straight Flush (1 HC). 1-
3 CD Inside Strt Flush (2 HC) 0.9+
4 Card Straight (1 HC)...... 0.9
3 Card Straight Flush (0 HC). 0.9-
4 Card Straight (0 HC)...... 0.8+
3 CD Inside Strt Flush (1 HC) 0.8
3 CD Dbl Ins Strt Flush (2 HC) 0.8-
Low Pair (2,3,4)............ 0.7+
Low Pair (5-10)............. 0.7
4 Card Inside Straight (4 HC) 0.7-
3 CD Dbl Ins Strt Flush (1 HC) 0.6+
3 CD Inside Strt Flush (0 HC) 0.6+
4 Card Inside Straight (3 HC) 0.6
2 Card Royal (No 10)........ 0.6-
3 CD Dbl Ins Strt Flush (0 HC) 0.6-
4 Card Inside Straight (2 HC) 0.5+
3 High Cards (No Ace)....... 0.5+
3 Card Flush (1 HC)......... 0.5
4 Card Inside Straight (1 HC) 0.5-
Ace......................... 0.5-
Two High Cards (No Ace)..... 0.5-
One High Card............... 0.4+
4 Card Inside Straight (0 HC) 0.4
3 Card Flush (0 HC)......... 0.4
RAZGU (Draw 5).............. 0.3+
```

PAY TABLE Per Coin; 5 Coin Play	FREQUENCY OF WINNERS

```
Royal Flush.......800 ...    1/  41,000
Straight Flush.... 50 ...    1/   9,100
4 of a Kind (Aces)160# ...   1/   4,200
          (2-3-4's) 80* ...  1/   1,900
          (5 - K)   50 ...    1/    600
Full House..........9 ...     1/     92
Flush...............6 ...     1/     88
Straight............4 ...     1/     78
3 of a Kind.........3 ...     1/     14
Two Pairs...........1 ...     1/      8
Jacks or Better.....1 ...     1/      5
   # 400 if w/ 2,3 or 4
   * 160 if w/ A, 2,3 or 4
Non-Winners  55%
```

PAYBACK: 98.8 %

On payback alone, "Double Double Bonus" leaves a lot to be desired, but it is certainly playing very strongly because it was the first to introduce a 400 payout on 4 Aces (with a 2, 3 or 4 condition). This is equivalent to half a Royal and many players just love to brag about such jackpots.

Unfortunately, the 9 / 6 paytable lulls players into thinking this game is played like 9 / 6 Jacks (JB-01) but one look at its long and complex strategy table should be a warning that playing it that way would be costly on many hands. A note: Don't hold Ace or 2,3,4 kickers with any key triplets

JB-25   Jacks or Better

```
Royal Flush................... 800
Four Aces w/ 2,3,4........... 400
Four Aces.................... 221
4 (2,3,4) w/A,2,3,4.......... 160
4 (2,3 or 4's)............... 100+
4 Fives to Kings............. 50
Straight Flush............... 50
4 Card Royal Flush........... 18+
3 Aces    (Bar 2,3,4)........ 13-
3 Aces    (w/ 2,3,4)......... 12-
Full House................... 9
3 of a Kind (2,3,4).......... 7+
Flush........................ 6
3 of a Kind (5-K)............ 5.4
Straight..................... 4
4 Card Straight Flush........ 3.5
4 Card Inside Straight Flush.. 2.3
Pair Aces.................... 1.9
Two Pairs.................... 1.7
3 Card Royal................. 1.5
High Pair (J-K).............. 1.4
4 Card Flush................. 1.2
Pair 2,3,4................... 0.9
4 CD Straight (1,2,3 HC)..... 0.8
Low Pair (5-10).............. 0.7+
3 Card Straight Flush (1 HC).. 0.7
3 Card Ins Strt Flush (2 HC).. 0.7
4 Card Straight (0 HC)....... 0.7-
4 Card Inside Straight (4 HC). 0.7-
3 CD Dbl Ins Strt Flush (2 HC). 0.6+
3 Card Straight Flush (0 HC).. 0.6
3 CD Inside Strt Flush (1 HC). 0.6
2 Card Royal (No 10)......... 0.5+
4 Card Inside Straight (3 HC). 0.5+
3 CD Inside Strt Flush (0 HC). 0.5+
3 CD Dbl Ins Strt Flush (1 HC). 0.5
3 High Cards (No Ace)........ 0.5
4 Card Inside Straight (2 HC). 0.5-
Two High Cards............... 0.5-
2 CD Royal (w/ 10 no A)...... 0.4+
One High Card................ 0.4+
3 CD Dbl Ins Strt Flush (0 HC). 0.4
4 Card Inside Straight (0 HC). 0.3+
RAZGU (Draw 5)............... 0.3
```

PAY TABLE Per Coin; 5 Coin Play		FREQUENCY OF WINNERS	
Royal Flush.......800	...	1/	40,500
Straight Flush.... 50	...	1/	9,300
4 of a Kind (Aces)160	...	1/	4,900
(2-3-4's) 80	...	1/	1,900
(5 - K) 50	...	1/	600
Full House..........8	...	1/	90
Flush...............5	...	1/	85
Straight............4	...	1/	90
3 of a Kind.........2	...	1/	13
Two Pairs...........2	...	1/	8
Jacks or Better.....1	...	1/	5
Non-Winners 55%			

PAYBACK: 99.5 %

On payback alone, "Double Bonus Plus" is much more attractive than other "double bonus" entries, but the subtle enhancement in paying two on Two Pairs but also 2 on Three of a Kind really does wonders for this version vis-a-vis the competitive "double bonus" games.

Most players go ballistic when just breaking even after drawing a pair to another pair (especially to a high pair). The chance of doing so is only 1 in 6 so it seems to them that some kind of reward should be forthcoming. This drawback is removed, albeit the Quad bonuses are toned down in the process. Even so, the "double your pleasure" theme applies to this game.

JB-26 Jacks or Better

```
Royal Flush...................800
Four Aces....................160
4 of a Kind (2,3,4)...........80
4 of a Kind    (5-K)..........50
Straight Flush................50
4 Card Royal Flush...........18+
3 Aces........................9+
Full House.....................8
3 of a Kind (2,3,4)..........5.7
Flush..........................5
3 of a Kind (5-King).........4.4
Straight.......................4
4 Card Straight Flush........3.4
Two Pairs....................2.5
4 Card Inside Straight Flush....2.2
Pair Aces....................1.8
High Pair (J-K)..............1.5
3 Card Royal................1.5-
4 Card Flush.................1.1
4 Card Straight (2,3 HC).....0.9-
Low Pair (2,3,4).............0.8+
Low Pair (5-10)..............0.8-
4 Card Straight (1 HC).......0.7+
3 Card Straight Flush (1 HC)....0.7
3 Card Ins Strt Flush (2 HC)....0.7-
4 Card Straight (0 HC).......0.7-
4 Card Inside Straight (4 HC)...0.6
3 Card Straight Flush (0 HC)....0.6-
3 Card Ins Strt Flush (1 HC)....0.6-
3 CD Dbl Ins Strt Flush (2 HC)..0.6-
2 Card Royal (No 10).........0.6-
4 Card Inside Straight (3 HC)...0.5+
3 High Cards (No Ace)........0.5+
3 Card Ins Strt Flush (0 HC)....0.5
3 CD Dbl Ins Strt Flush (1 HC)..0.5-
Two High Cards...............0.5-
One High Card................0.4+
3 CD Dbl Ins Strt Flush (0 HC)..0.4-
RAZGU (Draw 5)...............0.3+
```

JB-27 Jacks or Better

PAY TABLE Per Coin; 5 Coin Play		FREQUENCY OF WINNERS	
Royal Flush.......800	...	1/	40,000
Straight Flush.... 50	...	1/	9,300
4 of a Kind (Aces)400	...	1/	4,250
(2-3-4's) 80	...	1/	1,900
(5 - K) 50	...	1/	600
Full House..........8	...	1/	88
Flush...............5	...	1/	91
Straight............4	...	1/	80
3 of a Kind.........3	...	1/	13
Two Pairs...........1	...	1/	8
Jacks or Better.....1	...	1/	5
Non-Winners 55%			

PAYBACK: 99.8 %

"Super Aces" is an appropriate name for this game, which has the highest payline (yet) for 4 Aces without any special conditions. Recently approved for Casino Data Systems, the new video poker kid on the block, this game will find a wide audience among slot club players in its dollar version.

Note that an Aces Full hand easily gives way to a shot at the quad Aces, which brings home "half a Royal". Also, we don't hold another pair when we have a pair of Aces, but keep both pairs otherwise. Finally, we keep only the Ace if dealt an unmatched face card with it. Learn the strategy and this game can be "Super" for you.

JB-27 Jacks or Better

```
Royal Flush...................800
Four Aces....................400
4 (2,3 or 4's)................80
4 Fives to Kings..............50
Straight Flush................50
4 Card Royal Flush...........18+
3 Aces.......................20+
Full House.....................8
3 of a Kind (2,3,4)...........6+
3 of a Kind (5-K)............5+
Flush..........................5
Straight.......................4
4 Card Straight Flush........3+
Pair Aces....................2.4
4 Card Inside Straight Flush....2.2
Two Pairs....................1.6
High Pair (J-K)..............1.4
3 Card Royal.................1.4
4 Card Flush.................1.1
4 Card Straight (2,3 HC).......0.9
Pair 2,3,4...................0.8
4 Card Straight (1 HC).........0.7+
Low Pair (5-10)..............0.7
4 Card Straight (0 HC).........0.7-
3 Card Straight Flush (1 HC)....0.6+
3 Card Ins Strt Flush (2 HC)....0.6+
4 Card Inside Straight (4 HC)...0.6
3 CD Dbl Ins Strt Flush (2 HC)..0.6-
3 Card Ins Strt Flush (1 HC)....0.6-
3 Card Straight Flush (0 HC)....0.5+
2 Card Royal (No 10)...........0.5+
4 Card Inside Straight (3 HC)...0.5+
3 Card Ins Strt Flush (0 HC)....0.5+
3 High Cards (No Ace)..........0.5
Ace..........................0.5-
3 CD Dbl Ins Strt Flush (1 HC)..0.5-
4 Card Inside Straight (2 HC)...0.5-
Two High Cards (No Ace)........0.5-
2 Card Royal (Q/J-10)..........0.4+
One High Card................0.4
3 CD Dbl Ins Strt Flush (0 HC)..0.4-
4 Card Inside Straight (0 HC)...0.3+
RAZGU (Draw 5)...............0.3
```

KB-01   Kings or Better

PAY TABLE Per Coin; 5 Coin Play	FREQUENCY OF WINNERS

```
Royal Flush.......800 ...    1/  50,200
Straight Flush.....50 ...    1/   8,600
4 of a Kind.(A's).240 ...    1/   4,400
        (2-3-4)..120 ...    1/   1,900
        (Others)..75 ...    1/     630
Full House........11 ...        1/   95
Flush..............7 ...        1/   60
Straight...........4 ...        1/   80
Three of a Kind....3 ...        1/   14
Two Pairs..........1 ...        1/    9
Kings or Better....1 ...        1/    5
Non-Winners  65%
```

PAYBACK: 99.6%

This (Triple Bonus Poker) is the "sleeper" game in Las Vegas with its 11 on Full Houses. The strategy is so utterly simple and intuitive that almost anyone should be able to play like an expert with just a few minutes of instruction. Combine this payback with some type of slot-club awards and you can hold the casinos even over the long haul.

With the Kings as the minimum paying pair, the ranking table is stripped of all the pesky combinations of high cards and inside straight flushes, which clutter up most other games. Look at how short it is! Any fly in the ointment? Sure; just miss getting your share of Quads and you'll have a very short session at this machine.

KB-01   Kings or Better

```
Royal Flush...................800
Four Aces.....................240
Four 2-3-4's..................120
Four 5-Kings...................75
Straight Flush.................50
4 Card Royal Flush...........18.7
Three Aces...................13.6
Full House.....................11
Three 2-3-4's.................8.5
Flush...........................7
Three 5-K's..................6.6
Straight........................4
4 Card Straight Flush........3.7
4 Card Inside Straight Flush...2.5
Pair Aces....................1.9
Two Pair (Bar Aces)..........1.8
Pair Kings...................1.5
4 Card Flush.................1.4
3 Card Royal Flush...........1.3
Medium Pair (2-3-4's)........0.95
Low Pair (5-K's).............0.82
4 Card Straight (K high).....0.74
4 Card Straight..............0.68
3 Card Straight Flush........0.64
3 Card Inside Strt Flush.....0.53
4 Card Straight (2 HC).......0.47
3 Card Dbl Inside Strt Flush...0.45
Ace AND King.................0.44
Ace OR King..................0.40
4 Card Inside Straight.......0.34
RAZGU (Draw Five)............0.25
```

TP-01 Two Pairs or Better

PAY TABLE Per Coin; 5 Coin Play	FREQUENCY OF WINNERS

```
Royal Flush.....1,000 ...    1/  43,000
Straight Flush....100 ...    1/   7,500
4 of a Kind........50 ...    1/     430
Full House........11 ...      1/     90
Flush..............7 ...      1/     56
Straight...........5 ...      1/     61
3 of a Kind........3 ...      1/     14
Two Pairs..........2 ...      1/      8
Non-Winners  76%
```

PAYBACK: 94.0 %

This "vintage" Two Pair game is still available where there is little or no competition, or where the local authorities want to balance the budget. With a low payback and a short but difficult strategy, it is primarily for amusement. This game was one of the earliest casino offerings, designed to amuse the ladies while the men were at the Crap tables. Even the designers didn't know the true payback or the optimum strategy. Two pair games of all types, including Joker games never caught on strong.

It's important to make use of what little is dealt out, with many rag-tag hands (triple inside straight flushes, for example) being playable. In fact, there are no RAZGU's in this game. If a no "vig"double-down is offered, play it.

TP-01 Two Pairs or Better

```
Royal Flush...............1,000
Straight Flush.............100
4 of a Kind................50
4 Card Royal Flush...........23+
Full House.................11
Flush......................7
4 Card Straight Flush.........6-
3 of a Kind................5+
Straight...................5
4 Card Inside Strt Flush.......3.7
Two Pairs..................2.8
3 Card Royal Flush...........1.4
4 Card Flush...............1.3
Pair.......................0.9
4 Card Straight.............0.8
3 Card Straight Flush.........0.8
3 Card Inside Straight Flush....0.7
3 Card Double Ins Strt Flush....0.5
4 Card Inside Straight.........0.4
3 Card Flush...............0.4
2 Card Royal (J-10)..........0.4
2 Card Royal (Q-J,Q-10)........0.3+
2 Card Royal (K-Q,K-J,K-10).....0.3+
2 Card Straight Flush.........0.3+
2 Card Royal Ace High.........0.3
2 Card Inside Strt Flush.......0.3
3 Card Straight (=>5 High)......0.3-
2 Card Double Ins Strt Flush....0.3-
2 Card Triple Ins Strt Flush....0.3-
1 Midsize (3-Queen)..........0.3-
```

*Choose the Midsize Card which
has the most ways to create a
Straight and/ or Flush, i.e.,
at one end of a sequence and
with fewest discards in suit.*

TP-02 Two Pairs or Better

PAY TABLE Per Coin; 5 Coin Play		FREQUENCY OF WINNERS	
Royal Flush	1,000 ...	1/	46,000
Straight Flush	100 ...	1/	7,700
4 of a Kind	50 ...	1/	440
Full House	12 ...	1/	90
Flush	8 ...	1/	56
Straight	6 ...	1/	57
3 of a Kind	3 ...	1/	14
Two Pairs	2 ...	1/	8
Non-Winners 76%			

PAYBACK: 98.0 %

This "second generation" Two Pair game is still available and popular, with most machines offering a "no vig" Double Up option. Because all such DU's extend the playing time without affecting the bottom line win-loss results, they effectively reduce the House Advantage (1 - Payback) from 2% to about 1.6%.

Although the "Hit Frequency" is only 24% there are no pushes, a fact which many players favor, since they want to either win or lose, rather than spend time breaking even. Many players will play this game simply to have a shot at the DU feature, repeating the DU option until they (hopefully) end up with the gold ring or lose their bankroll trying.

TP-02 Two Pairs or Better

```
Royal Flush..................800
Straight Flush...............100
4 of a Kind...................50
4 Card Royal................19+
Full House....................12
Flush..........................8
4 Card Straight Flush........6.2
Straight.......................6
3 of a Kind..................5+
4 Card Inside Strt Flush.....3.9
Two Pairs....................2.9
4 Card Flush.................1.5
3 Card Royal Flush...........1.4
4 Card Straight.............1.0+
Pair.......................,,,,0.9+
3 Card Straight Flush.......0.9+
3 Card Inside Straight Flush....0.7+
3 Card Double Ins Strt Flush....0.6-
4 Card Inside Straight.........0.5+
3 Card Flush.................0.4+
2 Card Royal (J-10)..........0.4-
2 Card Royal (Q-J,Q-10).........0.4-
2 Card Straight Flush..........0.4-
3 Card Straight..............0.3+
2 Card Royal (KQ,KJ,K-10).......0.3+
2 Card Inside Strt Flush........0.3
2 Card Royal Ace High..........0.3
2 CD Dbl Inside Strt Flush......0.3-
2 CD Triple Ins Strt Flush......0.3-
1 Midsize (3-Queen)............0.2+
```

*Choose the Midsize Card which
has the most ways to create a
Straight and/ or Flush, i.e.,
at one end of a sequence and
with fewest discards in suit.*

J-01   Joker Poker

PAY TABLE Per Coin; 5 Coin Play		FREQUENCY OF WINNERS	
Royal Flush	800 ...	1/	41,200
Five of a Kind	200 ...	1/	10,700
Joker Royal	100 ...	1/	9,600
Straight Flush	50 ...	1/	1,750
Four of a Kind	20 ...	1/	120
Full House	7 ...	1/	65
Flush	5 ...	1/	65
Straight	3 ...	1/	60
Three of a Kind	2 ...	2/	15
Two Pairs	1 ...	1/	9
Pair K's or A's	1 ...	1/	7
Non-Winners 56%			

PAYBACK: 100.6%

This is the original full-pay game which, along with JB-01, propelled Las Vegas video poker to a new level of popularity in the 80's. After the initial surge, Joker games faded in L. V. to the point where only "downtown" casinos offer such high payers. While quite liberal, the strategy is more complex than most players can absorb so the crowds have drifted over to the easier non-wild games where equally liberal games are offered.

Key strategy points are: holding both pairs trying for a full house and picking a "midsize" card i.e., one in the range which is least adversely affected by the discards in suit or potential straights.

J-01   Joker Poker

NON-JOKER HANDS STRATEGY

```
Royal Flush................... 800
Straight Flush................ 50
4 of a Kind................... 23+
4 Card Royal Flush............ 20+
Full House.................... 7
Flush......................... 5
4 Card Straight Flush......... 4+
3 of a Kind................... 4-
4 Card Inside Straight Flush.. 3+
Straight...................... 3
Two Pairs..................... 1.6
3 Card Royal.................. 1.5
Pair A's,K's.................. 1.4
4 Card Flush.................. 1+
3 Card Straight Flush......... 0.7+
Pair.......................... 0.7+
4 Card Straight (K-Hi),,,..... 0.6+
3 Card Inside Straight Flush.. 0.6+
3 CD Dbl Ins Strt Flush (K Hi).. 0.6
4 Card Straight............... 0.6-
2 Card Royal Flush (A-K)...... 0.6-
3 Card Double Ins Strt Flush.. 0.5-
2 Card Royal Flush (A-x,K-x).. 0.5-
Ace AND King.................. 0.4+
Ace OR King................... 0.4+
2 Card Royal (no A,K)......... 0.3+
RAZGU Draw 5.................. 0.3+
```

JOKER HANDS STRATEGY

```
Five of a Kind................ 200
Wild Royal.................... 100
Straight Flush................ 50
Four of a Kind................ 23+
Full House.................... 7
4 Card Joker Royal............ 7-
4 Card Straight Flush......... 6+
Flush......................... 5
4 Card Inside Straight Flush.. 5-
4 CD Dbl Ins Strt Flu (K Hi).. 4+
3 of a Kind................... 4-
4 Card Double Ins Strt Flush.. 3.8
Straight...................... 3
3 Card Royal (King High).  ... 2.1
4 Card Flush (1 or 2 HC) ..... 2+
3 Card Royal (Ace Hi)......... 2-
3 Card Straight Flush......... 1.9
3 CD Tpl Ins Strt Flush (1 HC).. 1.8
3 Card Inside Strt Flush...... 1.7
High Pair..................... 1.7
3 Card Dbl Ins Strt Flush..... 1.6
4 Card Straight............... 1.5+
4 Card Flush.................. 1.5+
Joker + Midsize (5-10)........ 1.5-
Joker......................... 1.4+
```

73

PAY TABLE Per Coin; 5 Coin Play	FREQUENCY OF WINNERS
Royal Flush.......800 ...	1/ 43,200
Five of a Kind....200 ...	1/ 10,700
Joker Royal.......100 ...	1/ 9,600
Straight Flush.....50 ...	1/ 1,850
Four of a Kind.....20 ...	1/ 120
Full House.........5 ...	1/ 65
Flush..............4 ...	1/ 65
Straight...........3 ...	1/ 60
Three of a Kind.....2 ...	2/ 15
Two Pairs..........1 ...	1/ 9
Pair K's or A's.....1 ...	1/ 7
Non-Winners 55%	

PAYBACK: 96%

The waning interest in Joker games in Nevada quickly caused the removal of most of the quarter machines and replacement by nickels with degraded paybacks, such as the 20-5 game above. Apparently, the tourist traffic still has its love affair with Jokers, even low payers like this.

Key points in this complex strategy are: holding both Ace and King (discarding one reduces the value of the other; also applies to all other Kings or Better Jokers); play all two card Royals; hold both pairs trying for a full house (even though payline is only 5); "midsize" refers to the card within the range which is least affected by discarding which limit the formation of flushes and straights.

J-02 Joker Poker

NON-JOKER HANDS STRATEGY

```
Royal Flush....................800
Straight Flush.................50
4 of a Kind....................23+
4 Card Royal Flush.............19+
Full House.....................5
4 Card Straight Flush..........4+
Flush..........................4
3 of a Kind....................4-
Straight.......................3
4 Card Inside Straight Flush....3-
3 Card Royal Flush (No Ace).....1.6
Two Pairs......................1.4+
3 Card Royal Flush (with Ace)...1.4
Pair A's,K's...................1.4-
4 Card Flush...................0.8+
Pair...........................0.7+
3 Card Straight Flush..........0.7
4 Card Straight K-high.........0.6+
3 Card Inside Straight Flush....0.6-
2 Card Royal Flush (A-K).......0.6-
4 Card Straight................0.6-
3 CD Dbl Ins Strt Flush (K Hi)..0.5+
ACE AND KING...................0.4+
Ace OR KING....................0.4+
3 Card Double Ins Strt Flush....0.4+
2 Card Royal Flush (A-x,K-x)....0.3+
2 Card Royal (no A or K).......0.3+
RAZGU Draw 5 ..................0.3+
```

JOKER HANDS STRATEGY

```
Five of a Kind................200
Wild Royal....................100
Straight Flush................50
Four of a Kind................23+
4 Card Joker Royal............6+
4 Card Straight Flush.........6-
Full House....................5
4 Card Inside Strt Flush......5-
Flush.........................4
4 CD Dbl Ins Strt Flush (K-Hi)..4-
3 of a Kind...................3.8
4 CD Dbl Ins Strt Flush.......3.6
Straight......................3
3 Card Royal (with A or K)....2+
3 Card Straight Flush.........2-
4 Card Flush with/A or K......1.8
3 Card Royal (QJT)............1.8-
3 CD Tpl Ins Strt Flush (K Hi)..1.7+
4 Card Straight (K-high)......1.7
High Pair.....................1.7
3 Card Inside Strt Flush......1.6
4 Card Straight...............1.5+
3 Card Double Ins Strt Flush....1.5
Joker + Midsize (5-10)........1.4+
Joker.........................1.4
```

PAY TABLE Per Coin; 5 Coin Play		FREQUENCY OF WINNERS
Royal Flush.......800	...	1/ 40,000
Five of a Kind....200	...	1/ 10,800
Joker Royal.......100	...	1/ 9,600
Straight Flush.....50	...	1/ 1,700
Four of a Kind.....15	...	1/ 120
Full House..........7	...	1/ 65
Flush...............5	...	1/ 65
Straight...........3	...	1/ 60
Three of a Kind.....2	...	2/ 15
Two Pairs..........1	...	1/ 9
Pair A's or Kings...1	...	1/ 7
Non-Winners 56%		

PAYBACK: 96.3%

This "Kings or Better" version is another watered down remake of the original full-pay Joker Wild. Catering to the tourists who were raised on Joker games, the payback is too low to attract knowledgeable players to anything but nickel games.

With the advent of multi-game machines, the need for lots of new games has reincarnated "15-7" machines and raised the Quads to 17. This moves the payback up to 99% even on the nickel machines. The strategy is lengthy but the high pair payline eliminates the rag-tag types of hands seen in "two-pair" machines where comparable paybacks are attainable. (See J-04).

NON-JOKER HANDS STRATEGY

```
Royal Flush.....................800
Straight Flush..................50
4 Card Royal Flush.............20+
4 of a Kind...................19-
Full House......................7
Flush...........................5
4 Card Straight Flush..........4+
3 of a Kind....................4-
4 Card Inside Straight Flush.....3+
Straight........................3
Two Pairs.....................1.6
3 Card Royal..................1.5
Pair A's,K's..................1.4
4 Card Flush..................1.1
3 Card Straight Flush........0.7+
Low Pair......................0.7
4 Card Straight (K-High).........0.6+
3 Card Inside Straight Flush.....0.6+
3 CD Dbl Ins Strt Flush (K Hi)...0.6
2 Card Royal Flush A-K..........0.6-
4 Card Straight...............0.6-
3 Card Double Ins Strt Flush.....0.5-
2 CD Royal Flush (A-x or K-x)....0.5-
Ace AND KING..................0.4+
Ace OR KING...................0.4+
2 Card Royal (no A,K)..........0.3+
RAZGU Draw 5 ..................0.3+
```

JOKER HANDS STRATEGY

```
Five of a Kind................200
Wild Royal....................100
Straight Flush.................50
Four of a Kind...............19-
4 Card Joker Royal.............7+
Full House......................7
4 Card Straight Flush..........6+
Flush...........................5
4 Card Inside Strt Flush........5-
4 CD Dbl Ins Strt Flush K-high...4+
4 Card Double Ins Strt Flush.....4-
3 of a Kind....................4-
Straight........................3
3 Card Royal (K high)..........2+
4 Card Flush (1 or 2 HC).......2+
3 Card Royal (A or J High).....2-
3 Card Straight Flush........1.9-
3 Card Royal (Q High)........1.8+
3 CD Tpl Ins Strt Flush (K Hi)...1.8-
3 Card Inside Straight Flush.....1.7+
4 Card Inside Straight (K High)..1.7-
High Pair....................1.6+
3 Card Double Ins Strt Flush.....1,5+
4 Card Flush..................1.5
4 Card Straight...............1.5
Joker + Midsize (5-9)..........1.4
Joker.........................1.4-
```

J-04　Joker Poker

PAY TABLE Per Coin; 5 Coin Play		FREQUENCY OF WINNERS	
Royal Flush	1,000	1/	49,500
Five of a Kind	100	1/	10,800
Joker Royal	50	1/	13,500
Straight Flush	50	1/	1,700
Four of a Kind	20	1/	125
Full House	8	1/	70
Flush	7	1/	45
Straight	5	1/	35
Three of a Kind	2	1/	8
Two Pairs	1	1/	10
Non-Winners　69%			

PAYBACK: 99.1%

If you see this machine in the casino, it's very likely you are in Atlantic City, where "two-pair" Jokers are the meat and potatoes for the video poker fanatics. Although the most favored top payline there is Five of a Kinds, the Royal Flush is coming to the fore more visibly.

Players who dote on "two-Pair" games are well advised to stick to them exclusively, because the assortment of hands which are playable is unique to these machines. For example, 3 card inside straights and 2 card double inside straight flushes are worth playing in this game, but you won't find these rag-tag hands in most other games. When you see players at Jacks or Better holding these cards, you know where they are from and the problems they'll have.

NON-JOKER HANDS STRATEGY

```
Royal Flush.............1,000
Straight Flush.............50
4 Card Royal Flush.........23+
4 of a Kind................21+
Full House..................8
Flush.......................7
Straight....................5
4 Card Straight Flush.......5-
3 of a Kind.................4-
4 Card Inside Strt Flush.....3.5
Two Pairs...................1.7
3 Card Royal................1.6
4 Card Flush................1.5
4 Card Straight.............1-
3 Card Straight Flush.......0.9-
3 Card Inside Strt Flush.....0.8-
Pair........................0.7+
3 CD Double Ins Strt Flush...0.6
4 Card Inside Straight.......0.5+
3 Card Flush................0.4
2 Card Royal (Q or J High)...0.4-
2 Card Straight Flush.......0.4-
2 Card Royal (K High)........0.3+
3 Card Straight.............0.3+
2 Card Royal (A and K).......0.3+
2 Card Inside Strt Flush.....0.3+
2 CD Double Ins Strt Flush...0.3-
RAZGU Draw 5 ...............0.2+
```

JOKER HANDS STRATEGY

```
Five of a Kind.............100
Joker Royal (Strt Flu)......50
Four of a Kind.............21+
Full House..................8
Flush.......................7
4 CD Joker Royal (Strt Flu)..6+
4 CD Ins Joker Roy (St Flu)..5+
Straight....................5
4 Card Dbl Ins Strt Flush....4+
3 of a Kind.................4-
4 Card Straight (No Hi Cds)..2+
3 Card Straight Flush.......2-
4 Card Flush................1.8+
3 Card Inside Strt Flush.....1.8
4 Card Inside Straight.......1.6+
4 Card Straight (K high).....1.6+
3 Card Dbl Ins Strt Flush....1.6-
3 Card Tpl Ins Strt Flush....1.4-
3 Card Straight.............1.4-
Joker + Midsize (4 to J).....1.3
Joker.......................1.2
```

J-05   Joker Poker

PAY TABLE Per Coin; 5 Coin Play		FREQUENCY OF WINNERS	
Five of a Kind....	800 ...	1/	11,000
Royal Flush.......	100 ...	1/	63,000
Joker Royal.......	100 ...	1/	13,100
Straight Flush....	100 ...	1/	1,300
Four of a Kind.....	16 ...	1/	125
Full House.........	8 ...	1/	65
Flush..............	5 ...	1/	50
Straight..........	4 ...	1/	40
Three of a Kind.....	2 ...	1/	8
Two Pairs..........	1 ...	1/	10
Non-Winners 70%			

PAYBACK: 97.2%

This is the true original "full-pay" Atlantic City Joker machine and there are still hundreds of them, from old clunkers to high techs, found in most casinos.

The big attraction is the jackpot on Five of a Kinds, which occur much more often than natural Royals. Not many other locales have picked up on this game, but in LV these are almost always where the "double-up" players congregate.

The strategy is fairly complex with rag-tags abounding since RAZGU's are worth very little. That 70% failure rate weeds out the impatient, but those Quints keep them coming back for more.

J-05 Joker Poker

NON-JOKER HANDS STRATEGY

```
Royal/ Straight Flush.......100
4 of a Kind.................32+
Full House...................8
4 Card Royal/Strt Flush.......7+
4 Card Inside Strt Flush......5+
Flush.........................5
3 of a Kind.................4+
Straight.....................4
Two Pairs....................2-
3 Card Royal/Strt Flush.......1+
4 Card Flush.................1+
3 Card Inside Strt Flush......0.9-
4 Card Straight..............0.8-
Pair.........................0.7+
3 CD Double Ins Strt Flush....0.6
4 Card Inside Straight........0.5+
2 Card Straight Flush.........0.4-
2 Card Royal (no Ace).........0.3+
3 Card Flush.................0.3
2 Card Inside Straight Flush..0.3
3 Card Flush.................0.3
3 Card Straight..............0.3-
2 CD Double Ins Strt Flush....0.3-
2 CD Triple Ins Strt Flush....0.2+
RAZGU Draw 5.................0.2+
```

JOKER HANDS STRATEGY

```
Five of a Kind.............800
Joker Royal (Strt Flush)....100
Four of a Kind..............32+
4 CD Joker Royal (Strt Flu)..10
4 CD Ins Joker Roy (St Flu)...8+
Full House...................8
4 CD Double Ins Strt Flush....6-
Flush........................5
Straight.....................4
3 of a Kind.................4-
3 Card Straight Flush.........2+
3 Card Inside Strt Flush......2-
4 Card Straight..............1.7
3 CD Double Ins Strt Flush....1.6
4 Card Flush.................1.4
4 Card Inside Straight........1.4-
3 CD Triple Ins Strt Flush....1.4-
Joker + Midsize (5 to 10).....1.3+
Joker........................1.2
```

81

PAY TABLE Per Coin; 5 Coin Play	FREQUENCY OF WINNERS
Royal Flush.....1,000 ...	1/ 39,500
Five of a Kind....200 ...	1/ 11,000
Joker Royal.......100 ...	1/ 13,100
Straight Flush.....50 ...	1/ 1,700
Four of a Kind.....20 ...	1/ 120
Full House..........6 ...	1/ 65
Flush...............5 ...	1/ 55
Straight............3 ...	1/ 50
Three of a Kind.....2 ...	1/ 8
Two Pairs...........1 ...	1/ 9
Pair Aces...........1 ...	1/ 14
Non-Winners 70%	

PAYBACK: 94.3%

In response to the Las Vegas Kings or Better versions, the Taj in Atlantic City introduced a half-step game paying on Aces or Better. The payback is anemic, but the strategy for Joker hands is a tad simpler than that for the more liberal "two pair" and Five of a Kind machines.

When playing any one-joker game, we can expect the pre-draw hands to have a Joker only 9.5% of the time. In a one-card draw to a non-joker hand, only 1 in 48 will pull a joker. In a two-card draw, approximately 1 in 24 etc.

Joker games are for the very patient. The success rate is only 30% and only 40% of those improve the bankroll.

J-06 Joker Poker

NON-JOKER HANDS STRATEGY

```
Royal Flush...........1,000
Straight Flush...........50
4 Card Royal Flush.......24+
4 of a Kind.............24-
Full House................6
Flush.....................5
4 Card Straight Flush....4+
3 of a Kind..............4-
4 Card Inside Strt Flush...3+
Straight..................3
3 Card Royal............1.5+
Two Pairs...............1.5
Pair Aces...............1.4
4 Card Flush............1+
3 Card Straight Flush...0.7+
Pair....................0.7
3 Card Inside Strt Flush...0.6
4 Card Straight........0.6-
3 CD Dbl Ins Strt Flush...0.5-
2 CD Royal Flush A High...0.4+
Ace....................0.4+
2 Card Royal K,Q,J High...0.3+
4 Card Inside Straight...0.3+
2 Card Straight Flush...0.3+
3 Card Flush...........0.3
RAZGU Draw 5..........0.2+
```

JOKER HANDS STRATEGY

```
Five of a Kind ..............200
Wild Royal.................100
Straight Flush..............50
Four of a Kind.............23+
4 Card Joker Royal...........7-
Full House..................6
4 Card Straight Flush........6-
Flush.......................5
4 Card Inside Strt Flush....5-
4 CD Dbl Ins Strt Flush w/A...4+
3 of a Kind.................4-
4 CD Double Ins Strt Flush....4-
Straight....................3
4 Card Flush Ace High.......2+
3 Card Royal w/A or J-10....2-
3 Card Straight Flush.......1.8
3 CD Dbl Ins Strt Flush w/A...1.8
3 Card Royal Flush (Q High)...1.7+
Pair Aces..................1.7
3 Card Royal Flush (K High)...1.6
3 Card Inside Strt Flush...1.5-
4 Card Flush...............1.5-
3 CD Double Ins Strt Flush....1.5-
4 Card Straight............1.5-
Joker + Midsize (5-9),,,......1.3
Joker.......................1.2
```

PAY TABLE Per Coin; 5 Coin Play	FREQUENCY OF WINNERS
Royal Flush.......800 ...	1/ 38,000
Five of a Kind....160 ...	1/ 11,000
Joker Royal.......800 ...	1/ 8,800
Straight Flush.....80 ...	1/ 1,400
Four of a Kind.....25 ...	1/ 120
Full House..........5 ...	1/ 65
Flush..............4 ...	1/ 60
Straight...........3 ...	1/ 45
Three of a Kind.....2 ...	1/ 8
Two Pairs..........1 ...	1/ 9
Non-Winners 70%	

PAYBACK: 97.3%

This is a Minnesota game known as "Wild One" with dual jackpots on both natural and Joker Royals, a feature which has apparently remained in the "Land o' Lakes" to this day. The strategy is lengthy but players like those jackpots.

Key points of strategy: that 80 payline dictates that we draw to a triple inside straight flush (with Joker) and even a 2 card inside straight flush with no Joker; a three card Joker Royal outranks a Straight; a three card natural Royal outranks two pair hand; we never draw to a bare Joker.

J-07 Joker Poker

NON-JOKER HANDS STRATEGY

```
Royal Flush.............800
Straight Flush..........80
4 Card Royal Flush......34+
4 of a Kind.............27+
4 Card Straight Flush...6-
Full House..............5
3 of a Kind.............4+
4 Card Inside Strt Flush...4+
Flush...................4
Straight................3
3 Card Royal............2.6
Two Pairs...............1.4
3 Card Straight Flush...0.9-
4 Card Flush............0.8+
Pair....................0.7+
3 Card Inside Strt Flush...0.7-
4 Card Straight.........0.6-
3 Card Dbl Ins Strt Flu...0.5+
2 Card Royal Flush......0.4+
4 Card Ins Straight.....0.3+
2 Card Straight Flush...0.3
2 Card Inside Strt Flush...0.3-
3 Card Flush ...........0.3-
2 CD Dbl Ins Strt Flush...0.2+
Midsize (6 to J)........0.2+
RAZGU Draw 5 ...........0.2+
```

JOKER HANDS STRATEGY

```
Joker Royal.............800
Five of a Kind..........160
Straight Flush..........80
4 Card Joker Royal......34+
Four of a Kind..........27+
4 Card Straight Flush...8.3
4 Card Inside Strt Flush...6.5
Full House..............5
4 CD Dbl Ins Strt Flush...5-
3 of a Kind.............4+
Flush...................4
3 Card Royal............3.4
Straight................3
3 Card Straight Flush...2-
3 Card Inside Strt Flush...2-
3 CD Dbl Ins Strt Flush...1.5
4 Card Straight.........1.4
2 Card Royal............1.3
3 CD Tpl Ins Strt Flush...1.2
Joker + Midsize (4-9)...1.2-
```

85

J-08 Joker Poker

PAY TABLE Per Coin; 1-4 Coin Play	FREQUENCY OF WINNERS

Royal Flush.......500	...	1/ 38,000
Five of a Kind....500	...	1/ 11,000
Joker Royal.......500	...	1/ 9,200
Straight Flush.....50	...	1/ 1,800
Four of a Kind.....25	...	1/ 120
Full House..........7	...	1/ 65
Flush...............5	...	1/ 55
Straight............4	...	1/ 40
Three of a Kind.....1	...	1/ 8
Two Pairs...........1	...	2/ 19
Pair Aces...........1	...	1/ 14
Non-Winners 62%		

PAYBACK: 95.2%

This Louisiana track and truck stop game is a bit more liberal than its competitors, succeeding in a gallant effort to get as many jackpots on the table ($500.00 limit) as the law allows. The price exacted is to make a push out of triplets, which makes pushes out of 80% of the hands that manage to earn a payout. This quarter game flat-tops at 4 coins so any added coins actually reduce the payback.

With the premium awards on Joker Royals, the expert plays are: play a three card wild Royal in preference to a sure-winner 4 card flush (with Ace); draw to a midsize plus Joker, i.e., a card least affected by the discards, insofar as making flushes or straights is concerned.

NON-JOKER HANDS STRATEGY

```
Royal Flush................500
Straight Flush.............50
4 of a Kind................34+
4 Card Royal Flush.........22-
Full House.................7
Flush......................5
4 Card Straight Flush......4+
Straight...................4
3 of a Kind................4-
4 Card Inside Strt Flush...3+
3 Card Royal...............1.8
Two Pairs..................1.6
Pair Aces..................1.3
4 Card Flush...............1+
3 Card Straight Flush......0.7+
4 Card Straight............0.7+
Pair.......................0.6+
3 Card Inside Strt Flush...0.6+
3 CD Dbl Ins Strt Flush (w/A)..0.6
4 Card Inside Straight (w/A)...0.5
3 Card Double Ins Strt Flush...0.5-
2 Card Royal (Ace High)....0.4+
4 Card Inside Straight.....0.4+
Ace........................0.4+
2 Card Royal K,Q,J High....0.3+
2 Card Straight Flush......0.3
2 Card Inside Straight Flush...0.3-
3 Card Flush...............0.3-
3 Card Straight............0.3
RAZGU Draw 5...............0.3-
```

JOKER HANDS STRATEGY

```
Five of a Kind.............500
Wild Royal.................500
Straight Flush.............50
Four of a Kind.............34+
4 Card Wild Royal..........23+
Full House.................7
4 Card Straight Flush......6-
Flush......................5
4 Card Inside Straight Flush...4+
Straight...................4
3 of a Kind................4-
4 CD Double Ins Strt Flush.....3+
3 Card Royal...............2.8
4 Card Flush (Ace High)....1.8
3 Card Straight Flush......1.6
4 Card Straight............1.6
Pair Aces..................1.6
3 Card Inside Straight Flush...1.5
4 Card Flush...............1.3
3 Card Dbl Inside Strt Flush...1.3
4 Card Inside Straight.....1.3-
Joker + Ten, J,or Q........1.2
Joker + Midsize (K or 5-9)....1.2-
```

PAY TABLE Per Coin; 1-8 Coin Play		FREQUENCY OF WINNERS	
Royal Flush	250 ...	1/	57,000
Five of a Kind	185 ...	1/	11,000
Joker Royal	100 ...	1/	12,000
Straight Flush	50 ...	1/	1,750
Four of a Kind	20 ...	1/	120
Full House	6 ...	1/	65
Flush	5 ...	1/	55
Straight	4 ...	1/	40
Three of a Kind	2 ...	1/	8
Two Pairs	1 ...	2/	19
Pair Aces	1 ...	1/	14
Non-Winners 62%			

PAYBACK: 94.7%

This Louisiana track and truck stop version is a flat-top on Royals out to 8 coins, but adds a couple of mini-jackpots on the top rungs. Triplets are the most frequent winners in this game format and since they pay 2, while Quads pay 20, players have a reasonable chance to stay in play longer.

To illustrate the folly in passing regulations limiting jackpots and limiting payback, this is a true story. Some years ago a Blackjack game (payback 97%) accidentally was included in a multi-game machine in RI where a 92% cap applied. Players lined up to play it and the state was slow in removing it ---it made more money than the others.

NON-JOKER HANDS STRATEGY

```
Royal Flush.............250
Straight Flush...........50
4 of a Kind..............23+
4 Card Royal Flush........8.5
Full House................6
Flush.....................5
4 Card Straight Flush......4+
Straight..................4
3 of a Kind...............3.4
4 Card Inside Strt Flush...3+
Two Pairs.................1.5
Pair Aces.................1.4
4 Card Flush..............1+
3 Card Royal..............0.9+
3 Card Straight Flush......0.8-
4 Card Straight...........0.7+
Pair......................0.7+
3 Card Inside Strt Flush...0.7-
3 CD Dbl Ins Strt Flush....0.5
2 CD Royal Flush (Ace Hi)..0.4+
Ace.......................0.4+
4 Card Inside Straight.....0.4
3 Card Flush...............0.3
2 Card Straight Flush......0.3
2 Card Inside Strt Flush...0.3
3 Card Straight...........0.3-
2 Card Royal (K,Q,J High)..0.3-
RAZGU Draw 5..............0.3-
```

JOKER HANDS STRATEGY

```
Five of a Kind..........185
Joker Royal.............100
Straight Flush...........50
Four of a Kind...........23+
4 Card Joker Royal........8+
4 Card Straight Flush......6+
Full House................6
4 Card Inside Strt Flush...5+
Flush.....................5
Straight..................4
3 of a Kind...............4-
4 CD Dbl Ins Strt Flush....4-
4 Card Flush Ace High......2+
3 Card Royal Flush........2-
3 Card Straight Flush......2-
4 Card Straight(=< J High).1.8-
3 Card Inside Strt Flush...1.7
Pair Aces.................1.7
4 Card Straight(=>Q High)..1.7-
3 CD Dbl Ins Strt Flush....1.5+
4 Card Flush..............1.5-
Joker + Midsize (5-J)......1.4-
Joker.....................1.3
```

PAY TABLE Per Coin; 1-8 Coin Play	FREQUENCY OF WINNERS	
Royal Flush.......250 ...	1/	53,000
Five of a Kind....120 ...	1/	11,000
Joker Royal........80 ...	1/	11,000
Straight Flush.....30 ...	1/	2,000
Four of a Kind.....10 ...	1/	120
Full House..........6 ...	1/	65
Flush...............4 ...	1/	65
Straight............3 ...	1/	55
Three of a Kind.....2 ...	2/	15
Two Pairs...........1 ...	1/	9
Pair Jacks..........1 ...	3/	13
Non-Winners 46%		

PAYBACK: 94.7%

With a "hit frequency" of 54%, this Louisiana track and truck stop game acts more like a pinball than a Video Poker. Too bad 75% of the hits are just pushes. For sheer amusement, the action here is unsurpassed, almost like the Deuces and Joker versions.

What's more, its strategy is more like that of Jacks, with very few of those non-intuitive hands which torment players in other low payback games (two card inside straight flushes, for example) making it hard to learn.

J-10 Joker Poker

NON-JOKER HANDS STRATEGY

JOKER HANDS STRATEGY

PAY TABLE	FREQUENCY
Per Coin; 5 Coin Play	OF WINNERS

Royal Flush......800	...	1/ 45,000
Four Deuces.......200	...	1/ 4,900
Deuce Royal........25	...	1/ 560
Five of a Kind.....15	...	1/ 310
Straight Flush......9	...	1/ 260
Four of a Kind......5	...	1/ 16
Full House..........3	...	1/ 50
Flush...............2	...	1/ 60
Straight............2	...	1/ 16
Three of a Kind.....1	...	2/ 7
Non-Winners 55%		

PAYBACK: 100.6%

This is the original "full-pay" version of Deuces Wild, the game that really opened the floodgates to literally hundreds of games of all types which followed. Brought to the Las Vegas scene in 1987, it changed the basic nature of the game in Nevada, but has hardly made an entry elsewhere, except in versions offering much lower payback.

The players recognized the game's overly generous payback long before either the inventors or the analysts came to believe it. They quickly mastered its relatively easy strategy, sub-divided by the number of Deuces in the pre-draw hand. The mini-jackpot on 4 Deuces gave the players a totally new experience--a frequent recovery from a losing session. Streaky? Sure, but apparently tolerable.

DW-01　Deuces Wild

DEUCES

4	4 Deuces................	200
3	Royal Flush.............	25
	5 of a Kind.............	15
	3 Bare Deuces...........	15-
2	Royal Flush.............	25
	5 of a Kind.............	15
	Straight Flush..........	9
	4 of a Kind.............	6-
	4 Card Royal............	4+
	2 Bare Deuces...........	3+
1	Royal Flush.............	25
	5 of a Kind.............	15
	Straight Flush..........	9
	4 of a Kind.............	6
	4 Card Royal............	3+
	Full House..............	3
	4 Card Straight Flush...	2+
	3 of a Kind.............	2+
	Flush...................	2
	Straight................	2
	4 CD Inside Strt Flush..	2-
	4 CD Dbl Ins Strt Flush.	1.7
	3 Card Royal............	1.2
	3 CD Strt Flush (>6 hi).	1.1
	1 Bare Deuce............	1
0	Natural Royal..........	800
	4 Card Royal............	19+
	Straight Flush..........	9
	4 of a Kind.............	6-
	Full House..............	3
	3 of a Kind.............	2+
	Flush...................	2
	Straight................	2
	4 Card Straight Flush...	1.6
	4 Card Inside Strt Flush	1.4
	3 Card Royal............	1.3
	*Pair.(Bar 2-PR)........	0.6
	4 Card Straight.........	0.5+
	4 Card Flush............	0.5+
	3 Card Straight Flush...	0.5
	3 CD Inside Strt Flush..	0.4+
	2 CD Royal Q or J high..	0.4-
	4 CD Inside Straight....	0.3+
	3 CD Dbl Ins Strt Flush.	0.3+
	RAZGU draw 5 cards......	0.3+

DW-02   Deuces Wild

Sam's Town Twild

PAY TABLE Per Coin; 5 Coin Play	FREQUENCY OF WINNERS

```
Royal Flush.......800 ...    1/  44,400
Four Deuces.......400 ...    1/   4,800
Deuce Royal........20 ...    1/    600
Five of a Kind.....10 ...    1/    325
Straight Flush.....10 ...    1/    215
Four of a Kind......4 ...    1/     16
Full House..........4 ...    1/     40
Flush...............3 ...    1/     50
Straight............2 ...    1/     18
Three of a Kind.....1 ...    4/     15
Non-Winners   55%
```

PAYBACK: 101 %

Las Vegas is a "two upmanship" town, so the rush to Deuces Wild games had barely started when this "Double Pay Deuces" was launched. While everyone was sure that the payback would be lower than its generous predecesor, it turned out to be even more liberal. In a flash, most of them disappeared. However, Sam's Town kept them on as "Deuces Pay 2,000" and modified the game to make 7's wild, cutting the payback slightly.

With Quads showing up once in 16 hands (average), the loss of 1 unit on that payline reduces the payback 6%. Of course, the higher award on 4 D's offsets this, but the very streaky nature of all DW's is accentuated. As a result, many players find this liberal game too nerve-wracking.

DW-02 Deuces Wild

DEUCES

4	4 Deuces	400
3	3 Bare Deuces	23+
2	Royal Flush	20
	5 of a Kind	10
	Straight Flush	10
	4 of a Kind	5
	4 Card Royal	4+
	2 Bare Deuces	3+
1	Royal Flush	20
	5 of a Kind	10
	Straight Flush	10
	4 of a Kind	5-
	Full House	4
	4 Card Royal	3+
	Flush	3
	4 Card Straight Flush	3-
	4 Card Inside Strt Flush	2+
	Straight	2
	4 CD Dbl Ins Strt Flush	2-
	3 of a Kind	2-
	3 Card Royal	1+
	3 CD Strt Flush (>6 hi)	1+
	1 Bare Deuce	1
0	Natural Royal	800
	4 Card Royal	19+
	Straight Flush	10
	4 of a Kind	5-
	Full House	4
	Flush	3
	Straight	2
	4 Card Straight Flush	1.9
	3 of a Kind	1.8
	4 Card Inside Strt Flush	1.6
	3 Card Royal	1.3
	4 Card Flush	0.8
	*Two Pairs	0.7
	3 Card Straight Flush	0.6
	*Pair	0.6-
	4 Card Straight	0.5+
	3 Card Inside Strt Flush	0.5
	3 CD Dbl Ins Strt Flush	0.4+
	2 CD Royal Q or J high	0.4
	2 CD Royal K high	0.3+
	4 CD Inside Straight	0.3+
	RAZGU draw 5 cards	0.3+

DW-03   Deuces Wild

PAY TABLE Per Coin; 5 Coin Play		FREQUENCY OF WINNERS	
Royal Flush	800 ...	1/	45,400
Four Deuces	600 ...	1/	4,400
Deuce Royal	20 ...	1/	750
Five of a Kind	10 ...	1/	315
Straight Flush	8 ...	1/	210
Four of a Kind	4 ...	1/	15
Full House	3 ...	1/	40
Flush	2 ...	1/	50
Straight	2 ...	1/	18
Three of a Kind	1 ...	4/	15
Non-Winners 55%			

PAYBACK: 100 %

On the third try at cooling down Deuces, "Triple Pay Deuces" was created, a game which managed to get the payback down to 100% on the nose. This game immediately replaced Double Pay in most casinos, but even the inventors were shocked to find that it paid so much. Put this in a "slot club" casino and the players are ahead, so it naturally went as a proprietary game into the Station Casinos, which proudly proclaimed that they had no need for a slot club because they paid more out on their games.

In the final analysis, the players came out on top because the No Slot Club policy folded but the Triple Pay games remained and Double Pays simply moved to Sam's Town.

DW-03 Deuces Wild

```
DEUCES
  4   4 Deuces................600
  3   3 Bare Deuces...........31
  2   Royal Flush.............20
      5 of a Kind.............10
      Straight Flush..........8
      4 of a Kind.............5-
      4 Card Royal............4+
      2 Bare Deuces...........3+
  1   Royal Flush.............20
      5 of a Kind.............10
      Straight Flush..........8
      4 of a Kind.............5-
      4 Card Royal............3+
      Full House..............3
      4 Card Straight Flush...2.1
      Flush...................2
      Straight................2
      4 Card Inside Strt Flush...1.9
      3 of a Kind.............1.8
      4 CD Dbl Ins Strt Flush....1.6
      3 Card Royal Q or J High...1.1
      1 Bare Deuce............1
  0   Natural Royal...........800
      4 Card Royal............19+
      Straight Flush..........8
      4 of a Kind.............5-
      Full House..............3
      Flush...................2
      Straight................2
      3 of a Kind.............1.8
      4 Card Straight Flush...1.5
      3 Card Royal............1.3+
      4 Card Inside Strt Flush...1.3
      Pair..(Bar 2-Pr)........0.5+
      4 Card Flush............0.5
      4 Card Straight.........0.5
      3 Card Straight Flush...0.5
      3 Card Inside Strt Flush...0.4+
      3 Card Dbl Ins Strt Flush..0.4-
      4 Card Inside Straight....0.3+
      2 Card Royal Q or J high...0.3+
      RAZGU draw 5 cards......0.3
```

DW-04   Deuces Wild

PAY TABLE Per Coin; 5 Coin Play		FREQUENCY OF WINNERS	
Royal Flush.......800	...	1/	45,400
Four Deuces.......500	...	1/	4,700
Deuce Royal........25	...	1/	590
Five of a Kind.....17	...	1/	315
Straight Flush.....10	...	1/	210
Four of a Kind......4	...	1/	16
Full House..........3	...	1/	47
Flush...............2	...	1/	60
Straight............2	...	1/	18
Three of a Kind.....1	...	2/	7
Non-Winners 55%			

PAYBACK: 101.6%

The saga of the Deuces parade continued with this generous payout, which wasn't supposed to happen when the 600 for 4Ds became 500...but it did anyhow. There are a few still around but most have been "tamed" (slightly) by paying 15 on Quints rather than 17. Those are also called "Loose" as are some much lower like 12's with only 8 on Straight Flushes. So you see, the term "loose" also applies to naming poor payers after high payers.

When you note that a "profitable win" begins with a straight or flush, you begin to appreciate how streaky these machines can be. To realize the payback potential, one must be adequately bankrolled and must play maximum coins. A 500 coin bankroll will usually work out.

DW-04 Deuces Wild

```
DEUCES
  4    4 Deuces................500
  3    3 Bare Deuces............27+
  2    Royal Flush..............25
       5 of a Kind..............17
       Straight Flush...........10
       4 of a Kind..............5+
       4 Card Royal.............4+
       2 Bare Deuces............4-
  1    Royal Flush..............25
       5 of a Kind..............17
       Straight Flush...........10
       4 of a Kind..............5+
       4 Card Royal.............3+
       Full House...............3
       4 Card Straight Flush......2.4
       4 Card Inside Strt Flush...2.1
       Straight.................2
       Flush....................2
       3 of a Kind..............1.8
       4 CD Dbl Ins Strt Flush....1.8
       3 Card Royal (No Ace)......1.2
       3 CD Strt Flush (=>7 hi)...1.1
       1 Bare Deuce.............1+
  0    Natural Royal...........800
       4 Card Royal.............19+
       Straight Flush...........10
       4 of a Kind..............5+
       Full House...............3
       Flush....................2
       Straight.................2
       3 of a Kind..............1.8
       4 Card Straight Flush......1.8
       4 Card Ins Strt Flush......1.5
       3 Card Royal.............1.4
       3 Card Straight Flush......0.5
       Pair..(Bar 2-pr)...........0.5
       4 Card Flush.............0.5
       4 Card Straight..........0.5
       3 Card Ins Strt Flush......0.5
       3 CD Dbl Ins Strt Flush....0.4+
       2 Card Royal Q or J high...0.4
       4 Card Inside Straight.....0.3+
       RAZGU draw 5 cards.........0.3+
```

DW-05   Deuces Wild

PAY TABLE Per Coin; 5 Coin Play		FREQUENCY OF WINNERS	
Royal Flush.......800	...	1/	45,400
Four Deuces.......200	...	1/	4,900
Deuce Royal........20	...	1/	575
Five of a Kind.....10	...	1/	325
Straight Flush..... 8	...	1/	240
Four of a Kind......4	...	1/	16
Full House.........4	...	1/	40
Flush..............2	...	1/	60
Straight...........2	...	1/	17
Three of a Kind.....1	...	4/	15
Non-Winners 55%			

PAYBACK: 94.0%

While Video Poker is a mainstay in Nevada's casinos, it doesn't stop there. Operating with "restricted" licenses, which allow up to 15 machines in one location, the bars and supermarkets of Nevada also offer slot machines, with Video Poker usually dominating the scene. These machines are installed and serviced by route operators, who split the proceeds with the host location.

With the profits split two ways, and constant supervision required by the operator's coin clerks, the machines must take in more than their casino cousins to be profitable, so the pay tables are very tight and the paybacks are low. Many of the host locations are sorely dependent on the proceeds. Unfortunately, so are many of the players.

DW-05 Deuces Wild

```
DEUCES
  4   4 Deuces.................200
  3   Royal Flush..............20
      3 Bare Deuces............14-
  2   Royal Flush..............20
      5 of a Kind..............10
      Straight Flush............8
      4 of a Kind...............5
      4 Card Royal..............4
      4 CD Strt Flush (=>7 hi)...3+
      2 Bare Deuces.............3-
  1   Royal Flush..............20
      5 of a Kind..............10
      Straight Flush............8
      4 of a Kind..............5-
      Full House................4
      4 Card Royal.............3+
      4 Card Straight Flush......2.1
      Flush.....................2
      Straight..................2
      4 Card Ins.Strt Flush......2-
      3 of a Kind..............2-
      4 Card Dbl Ins Str Flush...1.6
      3 Card Royal..............1.1
      3 Card Strt Flush (>6 hi)..1
      4 Card Straight...........1
      1 Bare Deuce.............1-
  0   Natural Royal...........800
      4 Card Royal.............19+
      Straight Flush............8
      4 of a Kind..............5-
      Full House................4
      Flush.....................2
      Straight..................2
      3 of a Kind..............1.8
      4 Card Straight Flush......1.5
      3 Card Royal.............1.3
      4 Card Ins Strt Flush......1.3
      *Two Pairs................0.7
      *Pair.....................0.6-
      4 Card Straight...........0.5+
      4 Card Flush..............0.5+
      3 Card Straight Flush......0.5
      3 Card Ins Strt Flush......0.5-
      3 CD Dbl.Ins Strt Flush....0.4+
      2 Card Royal Q or J high...0.4-
      4 Card Inside Straight.....0.3+
      RAZGU Draw 5 cards........0.3+
```

DW-06   Deuces Wild

PAY TABLE Per Coin; 5 Coin Play	FREQUENCY OF WINNERS

Royal Flush.......800	...	1/ 44,400
Four Deuces.......200	...	1/ 5,200
Deuce Royal.......20	...	1/ 545
Five of a Kind.....10	...	1/ 330
Straight Flush..... 8	...	1/ 212
Four of a Kind......4	...	1/ 16
Full House.........4	...	1/ 38
Flush..............3	...	1/ 40
Straight...........2	...	1/ 17
Three of a Kind.....1	...	4/ 15
Non-Winners 55%		

PAYBACK: 96.0%

Midwesterners visited Las Vegas for many years, so it was natural for Deuces Wild to be an immediate favorite as the casinos opened in MN, IL, IA, IN, WI and MO. However the competition did not force the casinos to get into the wild melange of 100+% Deuces that set the standard in Video Poker Heaven. East Coast casinos have tended to follow Atlantic City's lead, where deuces wild machines are scarce and Jokers are rampant.

By raising the Full House payline to 4, the payback rises to over 96% even though the rest of the schedule appears anemic at first blush. The key play is keeping both pairs if dealt two pairs.

DW-06 Deuces Wild

DEUCES

```
4   4 Deuces................200
3   Royal Flush..............20
    3 Bare Deuces............14
2   Royal Flush..............20
    5 of a Kind..............10
    Straight Flush............8
    4 of a Kind..............5-
    4 Card Royal.............4+
    Flush.....................3
    4 CD Strt Flush (=>5 hi)...3+
    2 Bare Deuces............3-
1   Royal Flush..............20
    5 of a Kind..............10
    Straight Flush............8
    4 of a Kind..............5-
    Full House................4
    4 Card Royal.............3+
    Flush.....................3
    4 Card Straight Flush......2+
    Straight..................2
    4 Card Ins Strt Flush......2-
    3 of a Kind..............2-
    4 CD Dbl Ins Strt Flush....2-
    3 Card Royal.............1.2
    3 Card Strt Flush (=>6 hi).1+
    4 Card Straight (=>7 hi)...1
    1 Bare Deuce.............1-
0   Natural Royal...........800
    4 Card Royal.............19+
    Straight Flush............8
    4 of a Kind..............5-
    Full House................4
    Flush.....................3
    Straight..................2
    3 of a Kind.............1.8
    4 Card Straight Flush......1.7
    4 Card Ins Strt Flush......1.4
    3 Card Royal.............1.3
    4 Card Flush.............0.8-
    Two Pairs................0.7
    Pair.....................0.5
    4 Card Straight..........0.5+
    3 Card Straight Flush......0.5
    3 Card Ins Strt Flush......0.4+
    3 CD Dbl Ins Strt Flush....0.4
    2 Card Royal  J high.......0.4-
    2 Card Royal  Q high.......0.3+
    4 Card Inside Straight.....0.3+
    2 Card Royal K high........0.3+
    RAZGU draw 5 cards.........0.3+
```

DW-07 Deuces Wild

PAY TABLE Per Coin; 5 Coin Play		FREQUENCY OF WINNERS	
Royal Flush.......800	...	1/	44,400
Four Deuces.......200	...	1/	5,200
Deuce Royal........25	...	1/	525
Five of a Kind.....15	...	1/	315
Straight Flush..... 9	...	1/	230
Four of a Kind......4	...	1/	16
Full House.........3	...	1/	48
Flush..............2	...	1/	60
Straight...........2	...	1/	17
Three of a Kind.....1	...	2/	7
Non-Winners 55%			

PAYBACK: 94.3%

This is the "fooler" version of the classic full-pay Deuces, using a close (but very misleading) imitation of its pay table. The big bite is in the Four of a Kind payout, sliced to only 4 from 5 (for 1). The Frequency table shows that we can expect Quads about once in 16 hands. Voila, take away one bet unit each time and the player comes up short about 6%. Note that the payback is about 6% lower than on DW-01.

In Deuces Wild games the cut on Quads to 4 must be taken as a signal to pass the machine by, unless the 4 Deuces pay line is increased to at least 400. Players must always check the pay schedule carefully and cannot simply look for a game by its trade name.

DW-07 Deuces Wild

DEUCES
4	4 Deuces	200
3	Royal Flush	25
	5 of a Kind	15
	3 Bare Deuces	14
2	Royal Flush	25
	5 of a Kind	15
	Straight Flush	9
	4 of a Kind	5-
	4 Card Royal	4+
	4 CD Strt Flush (=>7 Hi)	3+
	2 Bare Deuces	3-
1	Royal Flush	25
	5 of a Kind	15
	Straight Flush	9
	4 of a Kind	5-
	4 Card Royal	3+
	Full House	3
	4 CD Straight Flush	2+
	Flush	2
	Straight	2
	4 CD Inside Strt Flush	1.9
	3 of a Kind	1.8
	4 CD Dbl Ins Strt Flush	1.7
	3 Card Royal	1.2
	3 CD Strt Flush (=>6 Hi)	1+
	4 Card Straight	1
	1 Bare Deuce	1-
0	Natural Royal	800
	4 Card Royal	19+
	Straight Flush	9
	4 of a Kind	5-
	Full House	3
	Flush	2
	Straight	2
	3 of a Kind	1.8
	4 Card Straight Flush	1.7
	4 Card Inside Strt Flush	1.4
	3 Card Royal	1.3
	*Pair.(Bar 2-pr)	0.5+
	4 Card Straight	0.5+
	4 Card Flush	0.5+
	3 CD Straight Flush	0.5
	3 CD Inside Strt Flush	0.4+
	2 Card Royal Q or J high	0.4-
	3 CD Dbl Ins Strt Flush	0.3+
	2 Card Royal (K high)	0.3+
	4 CD Inside Straight	0.3+
	RAZGU draw 5 cards	0.3+

DW-08　Deuces Wild

PAY TABLE Per Coin; 5 Coin Play	FREQUENCY OF WINNERS

Royal Flush.....3,200 ...	1/	38,400
Four Deuces.......200 ...	1/	5,200
Deuce Royal........25 ...	1/	500
Five of a Kind.....15 ...	1/	315
Straight Flush..... 9 ...	1/	235
Four of a Kind......4 ...	1/	16
Full House.........3 ...	1/	48
Flush..............2...	1/	60
Straight...........2 ...	1/	18
Three of a Kind.....1 ...	2/	7
Non-Winners　55%		

PAYBACK: 100.5%

This is the Progressive Deuces Wild game, shown at the point where the payback is equal to that of a full-pay game as shown in DW-01. Unfortunately, there are very few times when a player will find a jackpot at this level, but many novices think that the jackpot is attractive even at much lower values, because that is true of JB-02 games.

There is a big risk in playing these machines because the jackpot constitutes about 9% of the payback, so those who don't get the prize are playing at a heavy loss rate and must prepare to come in with a big bankroll. Therefore, it is likely that only "pros" will be taking all the seats when the machine offers a positive return. There are so many attractive DW games that you can afford to skip this one.

DW-08 Deuces Wild

```
DEUCES
  4   4 Deuces................200
  3   Royal Flush............25
      5 of a Kind............15
      3 Bare Deuces..........14+
  2   Royal Flush............25
      5 of a Kind............15
      Straight Flush..........9
      4 of a Kind............5-
      4 Card Royal...........3.7
      4 Cd Strt Flush =>7 hi.....3+
      2 Bare Deuces..........3+
  1   Royal Flush............25
      5 of a Kind............15
      Straight Flush..........9
      4 of a Kind...........4.9
      4 Card Royal..........3.7-
      Full House..............3
      4 Card Straight Flush......2.2
      Flush...................2
      Straight................2
      4 Card Ins Strt Flush......2-
      3 of a Kind...........1.8
      4 CD Dbl Ins Str Flush.....1.7
      3 Card Royal..........1.2
      3 Card Strt Flush (=>6 hi).1+
      4 Card Straight..........1
      1 Bare Deuce............1-
  0   Natural Royal.........3,200
      4 Card Royal............70
      Straight Flush..........9
      4 of a Kind............5-
      3 Card Royal...........4-
      Full House..............3
      Flush...................2
      Straight................2
      3 of a Kind...........1.8
      4 Card Straight Flush......1.7
      4 Card Ins Strt Flush......1.4
     *Pair...(Bar 2-pr)..........0.5+
      3 Card Straight Flush......0.5+
      4 Card Straight..........0.5+
      4 Card Flush............0.5+
      2 Card Royal (any)........0.5-
      3 CD Inside Strt Flush.....0.4+
      3 CD Dbl Ins Strt Flush....0.3+
      4 Card Inside Straight.....0.3+
      RAZGU Draw 5 cards........0.3+
```

DW-09 Deuces Wild

PAY TABLE Per Coin; 5 Coin Play		FREQUENCY OF WINNERS	
Royal Flush.......	800 ...	1/	44,400
Four Deuces.......	200 ...	1/	5,600
Deuce Royal........	25 ...	1/	550
Five of a Kind.....	16 ...	1/	320
Straight Flush.....	13 ...	1/	175
Four of a Kind......	4 ...	1/	16
Full House.........	4 ...	1/	48
Flush..............	3 ...	1/	57
Straight...........	2 ...	1/	18
Three of a Kind.....	1 ...	2/	7
Non-Winners 55%			

PAYBACK: 96.8%

This version made its debut in the high altitude casinos of Cripple Creek, Colorado and became so popular that the game also migrated to Minnesota. The tourists from those locales apparently became so enamored with it that the casinos in Las Vegas found it smart to import it, despite the fact that it has a much lower payback than its local competitors.

The high (13 for 1) payline on Straight Flushes skews our strategy to those partial straight flushes which show up at many levels. Playing expertly requires memorizing the ranks of these potential winners which comprise over 7% of our total payback

DW-09 Deuces Wild

```
4   4 Deuces.................200
3   Royal Flush..............25
    5 of a Kind..............16
    3 Bare Deuces...........14+
2   Royal Flush..............25
    5 of a Kind..............16
    Straight Flush...........13
    4 of a Kind..............5+
    4 Card Royal.............5-
    4 Card Straight Flush.....4-
    4 CD Inside Strt Flush....3.6
    4 CD Dbl Ins Strt Flush...3.3
    2 Bare Deuces............3.1
1   Royal Flush..............25
    5 of a Kind..............16
    Straight Flush...........13
    4 of a Kind..............5+
    4 Card Royal.............3+
    Full House................3
    4 Card Straight Flush.....2.9
    4 Card Ins Strt Flush.....2.5
    4 CD Dbl Ins Strt Flush...2.1
    Flush.....................2
    Straight..................2
    3 of a Kind..............1.8
    3 Card Royal (No A or K)...1.3
    3 CD Strt Flush (=>7 Hi)...1.2
    3 Card Ins Strt Flush.....1.1
    3 Card Royal (A or K Hi)...1+
    4 Card Straight...........1
    1 Bare Deuce.............1-
0   Natural Royal...........800
    4 Card Royal............19+
    Straight Flush...........13
    4 of a Kind..............5+
    Full House................3
    4 Card Straight Flush.....2+
    Flush.....................2
    Straight..................2
    3 of a Kind..............1.8
    4 CD Inside Strt Flush....1.8
    3 Card Royal.............1.4
    3 Card Straight Flush.....0.6
    *Pair..(Bar 2-pr)........0.5+
    4 Card Straight..........0.5+
    4 Card Flush.............0.5+
    3 Card Inside Strt Flush...0.4+
    3 CD Dbl Ins Strt Flush...0.4+
    2 Card Royal (Q or J Hi)...0.4-
    4 Card Inside Straight....0.3+
    2 Card Royal (A or K Hi)...0.3+
    RAZGU Draw 5 ...........0.3+
```

DW-10 Deuces Wild

PAY TABLE	FREQUENCY
Per Coin; 5 Coin Play	OF WINNERS

```
Royal Flush.......400 ...   1/  46,400
Four Deuces.......200 ...   1/   5,400
Deuce Royal........25 ...   1/    540
Five of a Kind.....15 ...   1/    320
Straight Flush.....11 ...   1/    190
Four of a Kind......4 ...   1/     16
Full House..........3 ...   1/     48
Flush...............2 ...   1/     57
Straight............2 ...   1/     17
Three of a Kind.....1 ...   2/      7
Non-Winners  55%
```

PAYBACK: 94.5%

These are found in Louisiana race tracks and truck stops.

The high (11 for 1) payline on Straight Flushes skews our strategy to those partial straight flushes which show up at many levels. Playing expertly requires memorizing the ranks of these potential winners which comprise over 5% of our total payback

Although the machine accomodates up to 8-coin play, the "cap" on payouts at $500.00 makes 5-coin play more cost effective. Like many low pay truck stop / race track games, it is tough to beat but much more liberal than reel-slots.

DW-10 Deuces Wild

```
DEUCES
  4   4 Deuces.................200
  3   Royal Flush..............25
      5 of a Kind.............15
      3 Bare Deuces...........14+
  2   Royal Flush..............25
      5 of a Kind.............15
      Straight Flush..........11
      4 of a Kind..............5-
      4 Card Royal.............4+
      4 Card Straight Flush....4-
      4 Card Inside Strt Flush....3+
      4 Card Dbl Ins Strt Flush...3+
      2 Bare Deuces...........3+
  1   Royal Flush..............25
      5 of a Kind.............15
      Straight Flush..........11
      4 of a Kind..............5-
      4 Card Royal.............3+
      Full House...............3
      4 Card Straight Flush.....2.6
      4 Card Ins Strt Flush.....2.2
      Flush....................2
      Straight.................2
      4 Card Dbl Ins Strt Flush...1.9
      3 of a Kind.............1.8
      3 Card Royal (No Ace).....1.2
      3 Card Strt Flush (=>6 Hi)..1.1
      3 Card Inside Strt Flush....1+
      4 Card Straight..........1
      1 Bare Deuce.............1-
  0   Natural Royal...........400
      4 Card Royal.............19
      Straight Flush..........11
      4 of a Kind..............5-
      Full House...............3
      Flush....................2
      Straight.................2
      4 Card Straight Flush.....1.9
      3 of a Kind.............1.8
      4 Card Inside Strt Flush....1.6
      3 Card Royal Flush.......1+
      3 Card Straight Flush......0.6
      *Pair.(Bar 2-pair).........0.5+
      4 Card Straight..........0.5+
      4 Card Flush.............0.5+
      3 Card Inside Straight Flush..0.5-
      3 Card Double Ins Strt Flush..0.4-
      4 Card Inside Straight......0.3+
      2 Card Royal (no A,K)......0.3+
      RAZGU Draw 5 Cards.........0.3
```

DW-11 Deuces Wild

PAY TABLE Per Coin; 5 Coin Play		FREQUENCY OF WINNERS	
Royal Flush	250 ...	1/	46,200
Four Deuces	200 ...	1/	5,500
Deuce Royal	30 ...	1/	540
Five of a Kind	20 ...	1/	320
Straight Flush	10 ...	1/	190
Four of a Kind	4 ...	1/	16
Full House	3 ...	1/	48
Flush	2 ...	1/	57
Straight	2 ...	1/	17
Three of a Kind	1 ...	2/	7
Non-Winners 55%			

PAYBACK: 94.5%

Although this machine can accommodate up to 8-coin play, the "cap" on payments at $500.00 makes 1 coin play most cost effective.

Like many low paying truck stop/ race track games it is tough to beat, but is still much more liberal than the reel-slots vying for your play. Games like this (and DW-10) should be considered only as forms of amusement, since the riverboats and Native American casinos present much better games

DW-11 Deuces Wild

DEUCES

4   4 Deuces...................200

3   Royal Flush.................30
    5 of a Kind.................20
    3 Bare Deuces...............12+

2   Royal Flush.................30
    5 of a Kind.................20
    Straight Flush..............10
    4 of a Kind.................5+
    4 Card Royal................5+
    4 Card Straight Flush.......4-
    4 Card Inside Strt Flush....3+
    4 Card Dbl Ins Strt Flush...3-
    2 Bare Deuces...............3-

1   Royal Flush.................30
    5 of a Kind.................20
    Straight Flush..............10
    4 of a Kind.................5+
    4 Card Royal................4-
    Full House..................3
    4 Card Straight Flush.......2+
    4 Card Ins Strt Flush.......2+
    Flush.......................2
    Straight....................2
    4 Card Dbl Ins Strt Flush...1.9
    3 of a Kind.................1.8
    3 Card Royal (No Ace).......1.2
    3 Card Strt Flush (=>6 Hi)...1.1
    3 Card Inside Strt Flush....1+
    4 Card Straight.............1
    1 Bare Deuce................1-

0   Natural Royal...............250
    Straight Flush..............10
    4 Card Royal................8+
    4 of a Kind.................5+
    Full House..................3
    Flush.......................2
    Straight....................2
    4 Card Straight Flush.......1.9
    3 of a Kind.................1.8
    4 Card Inside Strt Flush....1.6
    3 Card Royal Flush..........1-
    3 Card Straight Flush.......0.6
    *Pair.(Bar 2-pair)..........0.5+
    4 Card Straight.............0.5+
    4 Card Flush................0.5+
    3 Card Inside Straight Flush..0.5-
    3 Card Double Ins Strt Flush..0.4-
    4 Card Inside Straight......0.3+
    2 Card Royal (no A,K).......0.3+
    RAZGU Draw 5 Cards..........0.3

DW-12   Deuces Wild

PAY TABLE Per Coin; 5 Coin Play		FREQUENCY OF WINNERS	
Royal Flush	800 ...	1/	46,000
Four Deuces	400 ...	1/	6,100
Deuce Royal	25 ...	1/	550
Five of a Kind	16 ...	1/	325
Straight Flush	11 ...	1/	170
Four of a Kind	4 ...	1/	16
Full House	3 ...	1/	48
Flush	2 ...	1/	55
Straight	2 ...	1/	17
Three of a Kind	1 ...	2/	7
Non-Winners 55%			

PAYBACK: 99.6%

This version clearly illustrates the importance of examining the pay table rather than relying on the trade name of the game, because there are so many similar or identical names on different games. In DW-02 we strategized a game which was named Double Pay Deuces. This game is an imitation.

When players capitalized on the very liberal DPD, that game almost vanished and this game appeared in its place, easily fooling the careless players. However, it is a good game in its own right. The key is picking up on those partial straight flushes which comprise 5% of the payback. They are usually overlooked because they are not "playable" in games which don't reward straight flushes as well as this game does.

DW-12 Deuces Wild

```
DEUCES:
   4   4 Deuces................400
   3   Royal Flush.............25
       3 Bare Deuces...........23
   2   Royal Flush.............25
       5 of a Kind.............16
       Straight Flush..........11
       4 of a Kind.............5+
       4 Card Royal Flush......4+
       2 Bare Deuces...........3+
   1   Royal Flush.............25
       5 of a Kind.............16
       Straight Flush..........11
       4 of a Kind.............5+
       4 Card Royal Flush......4-
       Full House..............3
       4 Card Straight Flush...2.6
       4 Card Ins Strt Flush...2.2
       Flush...................2
       Straight................2
       4 CD Dbl Ins Strt Flush.1.9
       3 of a Kind.............1.8
       3 Card Royal (No Ace)...1.2
       3 CD Strt Flush (=>7 hi).1+
       3 CD Inside Strt Flush..1+
       1 Bare Deuce............1
   0   Natural Royal...........800
       4 Card Royal Flush......19
       Straight Flush..........11
       4 of a Kind.............5+
       Full House..............3
       Flush...................2
       Straight................2
       4 Card Straight Flush...1.9
       3 of a Kind.............1.8
       4 CD Inside Strt Flush..1.6
       3 Card Royal Flush......1.4
       3 Card Straight Flush...0.6-
      *Pair..(Bar 2-pr)........0.5+
       4 Card Straight.........0.5+
       4 Card Flush............0.5+
       3 CD Ins Straight Flush.0.5-
       3 Card Dbl Ins Strt Flush.0.4-
       2 Card Royal (No A or K).0.3+
       4 Card Inside Straight..0.3+
       RAZGU Draw 5............0.3+
```

DW-13 Deuces Wild

PAY TABLE Per Coin; 5 Coin Play	FREQUENCY OF WINNERS
Royal Flush.......250 ...	1/ 47,000
Four Deuces.......250 ...	1/ 5,000
Deuce Royal........25 ...	1/ 535
Five of a Kind.....18 ...	1/ 310
Straight Flush......8 ...	1/ 170
Four of a Kind......4 ...	1/ 16
Full House..........3 ...	1/ 48
Flush...............2 ...	1/ 60
Straight............2 ...	1/ 17
Three of a Kind.....1 ...	2/ 7
Non-Winners 55%	

PAYBACK: 94.6%

  This version is the only one anywhere which pays as much for 4 Deuces as for a Royal, but it still must contend with the cap of $500.00. We have to give the inventor credit for trying to make this Louisiana game interesting under those circumstances. The game should be played solely for amusement at the lowest denomination, since it is a "flat top" pay schedule. Note that we eliminate a couple of two-deuce pre-draw partial straight flush hands from the strategy because of the premium payout on the 4 Deuces and the minimal payout on Straight Flushes. Also, that we increase the number of 4-Deuce hands we win by this maneuver.

DW-13 Deuces Wild

DEUCES:

4 4 Deuces...................250

3 Royal Flush................25
    5 of a Kind................18
    3 Bare Deuces.............16+

2 Royal Flush................25
    5 of a Kind................18
    Straight Flush..............8
    4 of a Kind................5+
    4 Card Royal...............4+
    2 Bare Deuces..............3+

1 Royal Flush................25
    5 of a Kind................18
    Straight Flush..............8
    4 of a Kind................5+
    4 Card Royal...............4-
    Full House..................3
    4 Card Straight Flush.......2+
    Flush.......................2
    Straight....................2
    3 of a Kind................1.8
    4 Card Inside Strt Flush....1.8
    4 Card Dbl Ins Strt Flush...1.6
    3 Card Royal (No Ace).......1.2
    3 CD Strt Flush (=>7 Hi)....1.1
    3 Card Royal (Ace High).....1+
    4 Card Straight.............1
    1 Bare Deuce................1-

0 Natural Royal.............250
    Straight Flush..............8
    4 Card Royal................8-
    4 of a Kind................5+
    Full House..................3
    Flush.......................2
    Straight....................2
    3 of a Kind................1.8
    4 Card Straight Flush.......1.5
    4 Card Inside Strt Flush....1.3
    3 Card Royal................0.9
    *Pair.(Bar 2-pr)............0.5+
    4 Card Straight............0.5+
    4 Card Flush...............0.5+
    3 Card Straight Flush.,.....0.5
    3 Card Inside Strt Flush....0.4+
    2 Card Royal (J high).......0.4-
    3 Card Dbl Ins Strt Flush...0.4-
    4 Card Inside Straight......0.3+
    2 Card Royal (Q high).......0.3+
    RAZGU Draw 5 ....0.3

DW-14 Deuces Wild

PAY TABLE Per Coin; 5 Coin Play		FREQUENCY OF WINNERS	
Royal Flush	800	1/	44,000
Four Deuces	200	1/	5,300
Deuce Royal	25	1/	520
Five of a Kind	15	1/	320
Straight Flush	9	1/	200
Four of a Kind	4	1/	16
Full House	4	1/	38
Flush	3	1/	48
Straight	2	1/	17
Three of a Kind	1	2/	7
Non-Winners 55%			

PAYBACK: 98.9%

In the "Land of Lincoln" the Illinois casino players find a lot of high-paying VP machines, some even rivaling those found in Video Poker Heaven (Las Vegas). This one isn't quite that good but there aren't many better to be found outside of Nevada. The IL players will probably see the full-pay Deuces (see DW-01, DW-02 and DW-03) as competition heats up with Indiana, with full-pay Jacks and Bonus Pokers already installed.

A key play here is to keep both pairs and try for a Full House which pays 4 for 1. Note also that the partial flushes move up the strategy table since Flushes pay 3.

DW-14 Deuces Wild

DEUCES:

4	4 DEUCES.....................200
3	Wild Royal...................25
	5 of a Kind.................15
	3 Deuces...................14+
2	Wild Royal...................25
	5 of a Kind.................15
	Straight Flush..............9
	4 of a Kind................4.9
	4 Card Wild Royal...........4.8
	4 CD Strt Flush (=>7 High)..3.2
	4 CD Ins Strt Flush(=>7 hi).3.1
	2 Deuces....................3+
1	Wild Royal...................25
	5 of a Kind.................15
	Straight Flush..............9
	4 of a Kind................5-
	Full House...................4
	4 Card Wild Royal...........3.8
	Flush.......................3
	4 Card Straight Flush.......2.4
	4 Card Inside Strt Flush....2.1
	Straight....................2
	3 of a Kind................1.9
	4 Card Dbl Ins Strt Flush...1.8
	3 Card Wild Royal (No Ace)..1.3
	3 Card Strt Flush (=>7 Hi)..1.1
	3 Card Wild Royal (A Hi)....1+
	3 CD Ins Strt Flush(=>7 Hi).1+
	1 Deuce.....................1
0	Natural Royal.............800
	4 Card Royal...............19+
	Straight Flush..............9
	4 of a Kind................5-
	Full House...................4
	Flush.......................3
	Straight....................2
	3 of a Kind................1.9
	4 Card Straight Flush.......1.8
	4 Card Inside Strt Flush....1.5
	3 Card Royal...............1.4
	4 Card Flush...............0.8
	Two Pairs..................0.7
	3 Card Strt Flush..........0.6
	Pair.......................0.6-
	4 Card Straight............0.5
	3 Card Inside Strt Flush....0.5-
	3 Card Dbl Ins Strt Flush...0.4+
	2 Card Royal (No Ace).......0.4
	4 Card Inside Straight......0.3+
	2 Card Royal Ace high.......0.3+
	RAZGU Draw 5................0.3

119

DJ-01   Deuces and Joker Wild

PAY TABLE Per Coin; 5 Coin Play	FREQUENCY OF WINNERS
5 Wild Cards....2,000	1/ 130,000
Royal Flush.......800 ...	1/ 51,000
Four Deuces........25 ...	1/ 6,700
Deuce Royal.......12 ...	1/ 360
Five of a Kind..... 9 ...	1/ 180
Straight Flush......6 ...	1/ 135
Four of a Kind......3 ...	1/ 13
Full House..........3 ...	1/ 38
Flush...............3 ...	1/ 35
Straight............2 ...	1/ 15
Three of a Kind.....1 ...	2/ 7
Non-Winners 49%	

PAYBACK: 99%

This is the liveliest game ever invented, with 51% of all hands returning a payout, albeit more than half are pushes. There's lots of action but be warned that it is tough to walk away a winner because the big jackpots are few and far between. With many machines still pegged at the nickel level, DJW provides low-cost entertainment.

It's an easy strategy to master, since the hand values are concentrated at the lower values, which implies that an occasional error is not so costly as in most games. The most difficult part is interpreting each pre-draw hand properly. Some concentrated practice using the Glossary is likely to pay off well.

Wild:

5   5 Wild Cards........2,000
4   4 Deuces................66
    3 Deuces + Joker........52
3   Royal Flush.............12
    5 of a Kind..............9
    3 Wild Cards.............7-
2   Royal Flush.............12
    5 of a Kind..............9
    Straight Flush...........6
    4 of a Kind..............4-
    4 Card Royal.............3+
    Flush....................3
    4 Card Straight Flush....3-
    4 Card Ins.Strt.Flush....3-
    2 Wild Cards.............2+
1   Royal Flush.............12
    5 of a Kind..............9
    Straight Flush...........6
    4 of a Kind..............4-
    Full House...............3
    Flush....................3
    4 Card Royal.............2+
    4 Card Straight Flush....2
    Straight.................2
    4 Card Ins Strt Flush....1.8
    3 of a Kind..............1.6
    4 CD Dbl Ins Str Flush...1.6-
    3 Card Royal (Q or J Hi).1.1
    3 Card Straight Flush....1.1
    3 Card Royal (K or A Hi).1+
    3 Card Ins. Strt Flush...1+
    4 Card Straight.........1+
    4 Card Flush.............1
    1 Deuce or Joker.........1-
0   Royal Flush............800
    4 Card Royal...........19-
    Straight Flush...........6
    4 of a Kind..............4-
    Full House...............3
    Flush....................3
    Straight.................2
    3 of a Kind..............1.6
    4 Card Straight Flush....1.5
    3 Card Royal (Q High)....1.3+
    4 Card Ins Strt Flush....1.3
    3 Card Royal (A or K hi).1.3-
    4 Card Flush.............0.8
    3 Card Straight Flush....0.6-
    Two Pairs................0.6-
    One Pair.................0.5+
    4 Card Straight..........0.5+
    3 Card Ins Strt Flush....0.5-
    4 Card Inside Straight...0.4-
    RAZGU Draw 5.............0.3+

121

DJ-02   Deuces and Joker Wild

PAY TABLE Per Coin; 5 Coin Play		FREQUENCY OF WINNERS	
5 Wild Cards......500		1/	135,000
Royal Flush.......400	...	1/	54,000
Four Deuces.......100	...	1/	5,800
Deuce Royal........20	...	1/	360
Five of a Kind.....12	...	1/	180
Straight Flush......7	...	1/	135
Four of a Kind......3	...	1/	13
Full House..........2	...	1/	38
Flush...............2	...	1/	35
Straight............1	...	1/	15
Three of a Kind.....1	...	2/	7
Non-Winners 49%			

PAYBACK: 93%

This is the Louisiana version of the liveliest game ever invented, with 51% of all hands returning a payout, albeit more than two-thirds are just pushes. Somewhat like "kissing your cousin" gambling. There's lots of action but be warned that it is virtually impossible to walk away a winner unless one of the jackpots come your way. This version of DJW is strictly for amusement.

It's an easy strategy to learn because the hand values are concentrated at lower values, so an occasional error is not as costly as in most games. The hardest task is to interpret each pre-draw hand properly, especially the partial straight flushes, so practice with the Glossary will pay off.

Wild:

5 5 Wild Cards............500

4 4 Deuces................108+
   3 Deuces + Joker.........25+

3 Royal Flush..............20
   5 of a Kind..............12
   3 Deuces.................9+
   Straight Flush............7
   3 Wild Cards.............6-

2 Royal Flush..............20
   5 of a Kind..............12
   Straight Flush............7
   4 Card Royal (J,Q High)....4+
   4 of a Kind..............4-
   4 Card Royal (K,A Hi)......4-
   4 CD Strt Flush (=>7 Hi)...2.4
   2 Deuces.................2.4
   Deuce + Joker.............2.2

1 Royal Flush..............20
   5 of a Kind..............12
   Straight Flush............7
   4 of a Kind..............4-
   4 Card Royal.............3+
   Full House................2
   Flush.....................2
   4 Card Straight Flush......2-
   4 Card Inside Strt Flush...1.6
   3 of a Kind..............1.6
   4 CD Dbl Ins Strt Flush....1.5
   3 Card Royal.............1+
   Straight..................1
   3 Card Straight Flush......1-
   1 Deuce or Joker..........0.9

0 Royal Flush.............400
   4 Card Royal.............10+
   Straight Flush............7
   4 of a Kind..............4-
   Full House................2
   Flush.....................2
   3 of a Kind..............1.5
   4 Card Straight Flush......1.4
   4 CD Inside Strt Flush.....1.2
   3 Card Royal (Q or J Hi)...1+
   Straight..................1
   3 Card Royal (A or K Hi)...1-
   4 Card Flush.............0.5+
   Pair.(Bar 2-pr)...........0.5+
   3 Card Straight Flush......0.4+
   3 Card Inside Strt Flush...0.4
   3 CD Dbl Ins Strt Flush....0.3+
   2 Card Royal J-10.........0.3+
   RAZGU Draw 5..............0.3

PAY TABLE Per Coin; 5 Coin Play	FREQUENCY OF WINNERS

```
Royal Flush.......800 ...     1/  46,500
Joker Royal.......100 ...     1/   4,000
Five of a Kind.....50 ...     1/   2,400
Straight Flush.....25 ...      1/    650
Four of a Kind......8 (9)      1/     55
Full House.........5 ...       1/     55
Flush..............4 ...       1/     50
Straight...........3 ...       1/     30
Three of a Kind.....2 ...       1/      6
Two Pairs..........1 ...        1/     11
Non-Winners   63.7%
```

PAYBACK: 97.7%
100% if Quads pay 9

This game, played with a 54 card deck, can rightfully be called "The Pride of Atlantic City" because it originated there and is still very popular there. The NIH complex has kept it out of Las Vegas until now.

There are two versions of DJ that are worth playing. The more liberal pays 9 on Quads but is usually full up. The other pays only 8. A third "vacuum cleaner" version pays only 1 on triplets and should be avoided.

Pre-draw hands will show this distribution of Joker hands: None--82.18% ; One-- 17.12% ; Two--0.69% (1 in 140), so study that non-joker strategy carefully.

```
JOKERS
  0     Royal Flush................800
        Straight Flush.............25
        4 Card Royal Flush.........21+
        4 of a Kind................10-
        Full House.................5
        Flush......................4
        Straight...................3
        3 of a Kind................3-
        4 Card Straight Flush......2.7
        4 Card Inside Strt Flush...2.6
        Two Pairs..................1.5
        3 Card Royal...............1.2
        4 Card Flush...............0.9
        Pair.......................0.7+
        3 Card Straight Flush......0.7-
        4 Card Straight............0.6+
        3 Card Inside Strt Flush...0.6-
        3 CD Double Ins Strt Flush.0.5-
        4 Card Inside Straight.....0.4-
        2 Card Royal Flush.........0.4-
        2 Card Strt Flush (=>5 Hi).0.3+
        RAZGU (Draw 5).............0.3+

  1     Wild Royal.................100
        Five of a Kind.............50
        Straight Flush.............25
        Four of a Kind.............10-
        4 Card Wild Royal..........8+
        Full House.................5
        4 Card Straight Flush......4+
        Flush......................4
        4 Card Inside Strt Flush...3.6
        Straight...................3
        3 of a Kind................3
        4 Card Dbl Ins Strt Flush..2.9
        3 Card Royal...............1.7
        3 Card Straight Flush......1.5
        4 Card Straight............1.4
        3 Card Inside Strt Flush...1.3
        3 Card Dbl Ins Strt Flush..1.3-
        4 Card Flush...............1.2
        Joker......................1.1

  2     Royal Flush................100
        5 of a Kind................50
        Straight Flush.............25
        4 Card Royal (Q or J High).10+
        4 of a Kind................10-
        4 Card Royal (A or K High).9+
        4 Card Straight Flush......6+
        4 Card Inside Strt Flush...5+
        4 CD Double Ins Strt Flush.5
        4 CD Triple Ins Strt Flush.5-
        TWO JOKERS and 10..........4+
        Flush......................4
        TWO JOKERS.................4-
```

Glossary of Pre-Draw Hands

ROYAL FLUSH:		Ks Qs Js Ts As	Order is Not Important
Sequential	:	Ts Js Qs Ks As	Must be in Specified Order
	:	As Ks Qs Js Ts	Must be in Specified Order
Reversible	:	Both Above ok	No Wild Cards in Seqs and Revs
Joker	:	JJ Ts Ks Js As	Joker May Replace Any Card
Deuces (1)	:	D Ts Js As Ks	Deuce May Replace Any Card
Deuces (2)	:	D Ts D As Ks	Deuces May Replace Any Cards
Deuces (3)	:	D D D As Ts	Deuces May Replace Any Cards

4 CARD ROYAL:		As Ts Ks Js x	Missing Any One Card
Sequential	:	Ts xx Qs Ks As	Missing 1 Card from Sequence
	:	xx Ks Qs Js Ts	Missing 1 Card from Sequence
Reversible	:	As xx Qs Js Ts	Either Sequential OK
Joker	:	JJ Ts Js Ks xx	Joker May Replace Any Card
Deuces (1)	:	Ts D Ks Js xx	Deuce May Replace Any Card
Deuces (2)	:	D Ts Js D xx	Deuces May Replace Any Cards

3 CARD ROYAL:		As Js Ts x y	Missing Any Twe Cards
Sequential	:	Ts x Qs y As	Missing 2 Cards from Sequence
	:	As x Qs Js y	Missing 2 Cards from Sequence
Reversible	:	x y Qs Js Ts	Either Sequential OK
Joker	:	JJ Ts Js x y	Joker May Replace Any Card
Deuces (1)	:	Ts D x Js y	Deuce May Replace Any Card

2 CARD ROYAL:		Ks Js x y z	Missing Any Three Cards
Sequential	:	Ts x Qs y z	Missing 3 Cards from Sequence
	:	As x y Js z	Missing 3 Cards from Sequence
Reversible	:	x y z Js Ts	Either Sequential OK
Joker	:	JJ Ts x y z	Joker May Replace Any Card

STRAIGHT FLUSH:		5s 7s 6s 9s 8s	Five Card Straight in Same Suit
Joker	:	5s JJ 9s 8s 6s	Joker May Replace any Card
Deuces (1)	:	D 5s 9s 7s 6s	Deuce May Replace Any Card
Deuces (2)	:	D D 9s 7s 6s	Deuces May Replace Any Cards
Deuces (3)	:	D D 9s 7s D	Deuces May Replace Any Cards

126

Glossary of Pre-Draw Flush Hands (Continued)

4 Cd Straight Flush: 4s 5s 7s 6s x	4 Cd Straight Same Suit; No Gaps
Joker or Deuce: JJ 7s 5s 6s x	3 Cd Straight Same Suit; No Gaps
Deuce(2) : 5s D 6s D x	2 Cd Straight Same Suit; No Gaps

4 Cd Ins. Strt Flush: 6s 7s 5s 9s x	Single Card Gap
Joker or Deuce : JJ 7s 5s 8s x	Wild Card Fills In Single Gap
Deuces (2) : D 9s Js D x	Deuce fills Any 2 Gaps

4 Cd Double Inside Strt Flush:	**Must Have 1 or 2 Wild Cards**
Joker or Deuce: JJ 5s 9s 7s x	Wild Card fills in 1 of 2 gaps
Deuce (2) : D x 9s D 6s	Deuces fill in Both gaps

4 Cd Triple Inside Straight Flush:	**Must Have 1 Wild Card**
Joker or Deuce : JJ 5s 9s x y	Wild Card fills in 1 of 3 gaps

3 Cd Straight Flush: 4s 5s 6s x y	3 Cd Straight Same Suit; No Gaps
Joker or Deuce : JJ 5s 6s x y	2 Cd Straight Same Suit; No Gaps

3 Cd Inside Straight Flush: 4s 5s 7s x y	Single Card Gap
Joker or Deuce : JJ 5s 7s x y	Wild Card fills the Single Gap

3 Card Double Inside Straight Flush: 5s 6s 9s x y	Two Gaps
: As x 2s y 3s	**One Way to Fill**
Joker or Deuce: 4s JJ 7s x y	Joker fills 1 of 2 Gaps

2 Card Straight Flush: 7s 8s x y z (No Wild Cards)
2 Card Inside Straight Flush: 5s 7s x y z (No Wild Card)
2 Card Double Inside Straight Flush: 5s 8s x y z (No Wild Card)
2 Card Triple Inside Straight Flush: 5s 9s x y z (No Wild Card)